This book belo

Mr. Wendell Boyd

The Last Black Teacher
Race, Education, and Students of Color

The Last Black Teacher

Race, Education, and Students of Color

Wanda A. Alderman, Ph.D.

DEDICATION

I don' done what you told me to do
You told me to teach and I don' that too
I don' done what you told me to do...

Negro Spiritual (Howard University Choir, J. Weldon Norris, 1998)

This book is dedicated to every **Black Career Educator** in the known universe. Educators who create paths to resistance, design abilities for dreams, and leave no child without a vision.

The **Black Career Educators** in my life are truly the women in my family, the founders of my legacy. I dedicate this book to **Jannie Francis Ellis Cosby**, my maternal grandmother.

To members of **Alpha Kappa Alpha Sorority Incorporated**, my mother **Ruth Melba Dupree**, my aunt **Elizabeth Parker Cosby**, my cousin **Mary Jackson Ellis**, the first Black certified teacher in the state of Minnesota, and her daughter **Joy Ellis Bartlett,** who is genuinely a perfect teacher—thank you for exemplifying excellence in teaching.

And, to my father **Marion Alderman**, who I miss every day.

Last, to **Stafford Alderman Swain**, who taught Santana that summers and water are forever.

CONTENTS

ACKNOWLEDGMENTS

Finding words and capturing moments for this book meant spending hours, days, and life in solitude—every topic created another topic and required hours of research and philosophical reflections. Authoring a book is a tedious process--made shorter by the tremendous amount of support from family and friends.

Without the support of my husband, Melvin L. Swain, I would not have eaten lunch and laughed. My sons, Brandon Alderman Swain and Dominic Alderman Swain, were patient with my journey but never allowed me to exist alone in the universe. They required daily interactions with my scrambled thoughts. They answered my tangled questions—for example, why is paper white and ink black...what if the paper was black and the ink was white?

Thank you to my neighbors Euzell Powell and Ralph Jackson, who provided continuous support and encouragement. Thank you to my friends Gloria Allen,Mary Keets Jay, and Drs. Joan Jackson and Regina Young. I am forever appreciative.

To Dr. Robert M. Brown III, I am thankful for your time, scholarly advice, support, and friendship. You are indeed my Alpha Brother.

Last—every author's wish, a marvelous editor—thank you Donna Pintek.

PREFACE

From Drug Dealers to Death Drills...

According to W. E. B. Du Bois....

"Take for instance the current problem of the education of our children. By the law of the land today they should be admitted to the public schools. If and when they are admitted to these schools certain things will inevitably follow. Negro teachers will become rarer and in many cases will disappear. Negro children will be instructed in the public schools and taught under unpleasant if not discouraging circumstances. Even more largely than today they will fall out of school, cease to enter high school, and fewer and fewer will go to college. Theoretically, Negro universities will disappear. Negro history will be taught less or not at all, and as in so many cases in the past Negroes will remember their white or Indian ancestors and quite forget their Negro forebearers." (Whither Now and Why, 1960) (From Aptheker, 1973).

Race

Since *Brown v. The Board of Education of Topeka, Kansas* in 1954, the resistance to desegregation required additional race-based policies, ideologies, and practices related to deficit thinking—an ideology that supported the belief that students of color were inferior, and school funding and resources were better utilized in white school districts where students exhibited higher academic achievements, especially on standardized tests.

Racism is systemic and a permanent fixture in America's institutions. A social construct, racism is concurrent with life for all individuals of color to maintain white supremacy, whiteness, white dominance, and white power.

Public schools are an institution in our society and they are supported by systemic racism with the use of inequalities—inequalities that manifest as resegregation, the lack of school funding, the lack of school resources, biased standardized testing, criminalization in the schoolhouse, marginalization within schools, and curriculums and pedagogy that fail to teach skills linked to the future of work for students of color.

Sixty-six years after *Brown*, public education for students of color (Black and Hispanic) provides a permanent highway to prison pipelines, unemployment, underemployment, and school curricula devoid of skills for life-sustaining employment and well-being in global and technology-driven economies.

In 1954, the resistance to desegregation in public schools provided psychologically damaging interactions that affected Black students' personal and professional life experiences. Today, with the permanence of social, economic, and political racialized tools, students of color experience an increase in mental health issues. Evidence shows that racial disparities in suicide rates for Black children ages 5-12 are two times higher than those of similarly aged children. Overall, experiences with racism impact a child's cognitive and social development. With health care disparities, children of color illustrate that their encounters with mental health issues are increasing and not likely to be addressed by professionals.

Students of color attend schools that fail to meet the minimum staffing recommendations for school-based mental health providers. In contrast, law enforcement in most public schools has a far more significant presence—a presence that leads to more chances of being detained, handcuffed, and arrested in the schoolhouse.

The resistance to *Brown* was enhanced by permanently destroying the legacy of Black Career Educators who, at the dawn of both *Brown I and Brown II*, faced discrimination, racism, prejudice, and the elimination of jobs. With racialized economic and political policies, and laws, their teaching careers were devastated as white teachers with fewer qualifications took their jobs, and white public schools refused to stain their classrooms by hiring "Negro" educators. Opportunities for Black Career Educators to continue their professional journeys, during the pretense of desegregation, were removed from the nation's agenda.

Black Career Educators who continued to teach were often isolated in urban and rural school districts. However, by 2008, they represented 16 percent of public school educators. Today, Black Career Educators represent only 7 percent of public school teachers, the majority are female, and less than 2 percent are men. As the majority of Black Career Educators retire, Black and Hispanic students are left without advocates for education equality.

Instead, students of color will enter classrooms, where 80 percent of the current teaching population in America is white and mostly female. If this population of educators fails to embrace a student's racial and cultural identity or recognize the influence of racial inequalities in student achievement, then students of color will attend public schools devoid of culturally relevant pedagogy, drenched in deficit thinking, and framed in structural racism.

Education

After thirty-six years in both secondary and collegiate educational environments, I share with you in living color the chaos and social psychological impact of race, teaching, instructing students of color, and teaching while Black in America. In the 1980s, I dodged bullets, stepped over dead bodies to get in my car, instructed 15-year-old drug dealers, knew students who were murderers, witnessed students who were shot while standing next to me, and experienced the death of countless former students. As I exit the schoolhouse, drug dealers have been replaced with death drills—the art of preparing teachers and students for gun violence in the schoolhouse.

As a Black Career Educator, my career is not a single journey. There are thousands of Black Career Educators, and our career journeys must be written and framed in the context of America's structural racism that systemically removed and marginalized our professional journeys. The mere presence of Black educators created a violent response enforced by laws and policies to imply that we were unsuitable, unlicensed, inexperienced, and by no means could be placed in a classroom with white students, for we were barely qualified to instruct Black children.

Society was not interested in our teaching philosophy or values and beliefs about the purpose of education. Instead, society questioned our dedication, qualifications, and distorted perceptions about our professionalism. Thus, our careers must be written, discussed, and framed. Our travels through the schoolhouse must be mounted in the context of America's structural design that systemically removed, disenfranchised, and marginalized our professionalism.

Changes in school culture and climate are linked to social evolutions. The free use of curse words in the hallways and classrooms, cursing at teachers, and the overall removal of civility impacts school cultures and climates, which are causally linked to the social, psychological, and cultural changes in society. Students balance between enculturation and acculturation, especially violent behaviors utilized to solve the smallest conflicts. With changes in school culture and climates, teacher victimization is one of the most underreported topics, and the study of violence towards teachers is new. Some scholars believe that nationwide, 80 percent of teachers experience at least one act of victimization in a school year. Teacher victimization, like mental illness, is a global issue, widespread, and includes disruptive behaviors, cyberbullying, sexual assaults, and parent and administrative bullying of teachers.

The use of marijuana in public schools is not uncommon, regardless of grade level. Depending on the school district's location, the penalty for bringing and using marijuana on school property varies. Unlike most professional work environments, exposure to marijuana in schools is levitating without consequences or regard to maintaining a safe environment for teachers, students, and other professionals.

As if nothing has changed since 1954, racialized perceptions dismantle economic and educational opportunities for people of color. When Blacks escape urban poverty, Black middle-class suburban enclaves are destroyed by racist housing policies, predatory loans, and the continuation of educational inequalities. Conditions that extend beyond the control of the Black middle-class in suburban enclaves but are reflective of racist policies that destroy opportunities for their children to obtain equality in education and for Black families to build generational wealth, especially as the wealth gap between white families and families of color dramatically increases each year.

The lives of Black and Hispanic children coexist with prejudice, discrimination, racism, food insecurity, and academic oppression in their resegregated schools and isolated communities. These conditions affect their self- worth, and of course, their mental health outcomes. Combine this data with the fact that more and more children of color live in communities with high rates of poverty, segregated housing, and attend resegregated public schools that do not provide transitional skills to post-secondary education, careers, and the future of work.

As Black scholars entered the halls of higher education and racially integrated teaching environments, they were reminded that they are teaching while Black. In the year 2020, Black scholars teaching at predominately white institutions are abused by white students and colleagues who question their credentials, research focus, and ability to instruct white students. White university administrators ignore racial abuse towards Black professors as if it occurs on campus and does not circulate to the national news media—a campus secret. Thus, reprehensible race-based behaviors directed towards professors of color create hostile academic atmospheres, and it is far easier to assume that Black faculty members are a problem than to address the underlying racism within predominantly white institutions.

Students of Color

I am a Black Career Educator, and collectively, we represent the largest population of educators of color in the United States. However, during the next five years, some 10,000 educators in the United States will retire daily. As for Black Career Educators, no one will replace us, and the majority population in public schools, students of color, will lose their only exponents for equality in public education and interpreters of culturally relevant pedagogy. When educators of color are present, students of color are given the ambition to achieve, to see themselves as leaders, and have someone to explain the microaggressions of racism. Educators of color provide distinctive styles related to student outcomes, pedagogy, and cannot be replaced by individuals who once completed a course in diversity and education.

Students of color will enter classrooms with educators who complete teacher education programs devoid of courses related to race, diversity, and cultural pedagogy. White middle-class teachers will have a significant cultural disconnect with students of color in public schools and, thus, perpetuate white supremacy, deficit thinking, and economic inequity. Without a focus on social or racial justice in teacher education programs, teachers are not prepared to understand the significance of race and racism as it relates to students of color, their families, and their communities.

Resegregation and education inequality has intensified in the twenty-first century. The experiment with *Brown* created new tools to support white dominance and white power but could not counter-act white supremacy to achieve education equality in America. White student enrollment in public schools has declined, and the number of white births has declined. Yet, the resegregation of students of color assures that they will not attend integrated schools or receive an education for life-sustaining employment and well-being.

New racist tools enforced by federal and public education policies include dismantling the federally supported Free and Reduced Meals Program (FARMs), and The Supplemental Nutrition Assistance Program (SNAP), formerly known as food stamps. Students of color who live in urban cities attend public schools where most of their classmates live in poverty or with low-income families. This data indicates that the systemic impact of racism dismantles quality education for students of color, given the correlation with poverty and low educational achievement.

As the wealth gap between whites and families of color increases, the majority of local school district funding is often directed towards predominately white school communities. This data coincides with the fact that most school districts in America are not equipped to address demographic and economic changes in their school population with adequate resources. With the use of new racist tools, school districts may require students of color to pay for their secondary education providing they meet the demands of education policies designed to remove them from public education and permanently from the workforce. If the majority population of students in public schools (Blacks and Hispanics) fails to meet the demands of new raced-based policies and standards, their parents will be offered an option to pay-out-of-pocket for their child to attend public schools. The nature of institutional racism advances the Apartheid nature of the current public education system in the United States. Thus, from K-12, students of color are marginalized by racialized policies and practices that are designed to disrupt their academic potential and feed them into prisons, low-wage jobs, and permanent underemployment.

I invite you to follow me on Facebook, Twitter, Instagram, and at www.lastblackteacher.com

1 THE ART AND SCIENCE OF TEACHING

Innate Skills

The art of teaching extends beyond individuals who possess a set of innate skills, depart knowledge to captive audiences, or create magical experiences for students. Possessing knowledge, techniques, and integrity does not define teaching, nor can teachers assume that a student's ability to learn is innate.

Some educators argue that teaching developed as a science. This ideology naturally aligns teaching with practices that build confidence while trying a variety of practical approaches to teaching. Whether viewing teaching as an art or science, the reality of teaching assumes all student outcomes and teacher abilities to be effective.

In 1986, David Berliner described teaching as a mixture of expertise and instructional strategies that may enlighten a student's understanding. However, a teacher must determine which strategies are most effective while combining both the art and science of teaching. Research recognizes a variety of instructional strategies, as no one approach to teaching works for every student who enters a classroom. Teaching encompasses a variety of strategies that, on any given day, have a probability of working or not working.

Some education reformers indicate that great teachers are made and not born. However, the difficulty arises in determining which life and career experiences cultivate great teachers. No one is born to teach, to impart knowledge, and can determine if another individual who encounters an academic persona somehow, magically, leaves with skills and knowledge. Correlation between a teacher's innate characteristics and student achievement is non-existent. As the United States encounters a significant shortage of educators, a random list of innate skills will not determine a teacher's probability of success.

Finding your niche, whether it is elementary, middle, or the high school level, is not linked to innate qualities such as caring, having patience, passion, humor, and creativity, speaking encouraging words, or displaying a joyous personality in the classroom. Determining a grade level or grade range to teach is a crucial decision and a more prodigious decision for teachers. This decision needs to take into consideration knowledge, training, expertise, and teaching style to determine the best classroom environment and to succeed at meeting desired expectations for student growth.

In philosophy, the innatism doctrine says our mind arrives pre-packaged with ideas, knowledge, and beliefs at birth, and not all knowledge formulates from one's senses and experiences in the environment (Stewart & Blocker, 2012). Moreover, while our interactions with our environment are essential, environments are not the only source of knowledge.

Plato offered an idea that if everything we perceive as having beauty vanished, would beauty still exist? Thus, he supported a belief that both innate concepts and knowledge exist independently. Like Plato's argument for the existence of beauty, if teachers did not have innate qualities, would students still acquire knowledge?

Scientific studies prove that innate knowledge does exist, especially basic knowledge inscribed in our DNA. However, there is a balance between what we acquire through life experiences and what our genes express. As for the art of teaching and students gaining knowledge, both are independent of a teacher's innate qualities.

Some educators insist that all teachers must have a collective group of innate qualities to be effective, and every incredible teacher must love children or consider another profession. After 35 years of teaching, I barely have enough love for my family members, and I am guarded about loving 170 strangers who enter a classroom every year. Instead, I would rather learn their names, plan for a successful school year, and find an engaging teaching strategy that inspires teaching and students to value knowledge and skills associated with a lesson.

The Art and Science of Teaching

Robert Marzano wrote *The Art and Science of Teaching* (2007) to illustrate the necessary balance between research-based data and understanding the strengths and weaknesses of individual students. Marzano supports the concept of using instructional strategies based on science and research and asserts that mastering the art of knowing when and with whom to use these strategies supports excellence in teaching. Using multiple questions to design a logical planning sequence for active learning, Marzano articulates that teachers must evaluate 10 components of their teaching process using a variety of organizers, rubrics, and charts to develop their knowledge and skills methodically. The process leads to integrating the science and art of teaching, developing exceptional teaching, and ensuring amazing student achievements.

In July 2019, Marzano commented that a student's attention and engagement are directly under the control of the classroom teacher, and there is no reason any student should be systematically bored, inattentive, or disengaged in any class at any grade level. Naturally, career educators did not agree with Marzano's comments. Marzano presents the nature of teaching as a set of instructions for assembling furniture and aligns teaching with technical approaches to learning established by research-based teaching practices. Marzano's comments, in general, reflect someone removed from the realities of teaching in public schools, as well as individuals with minimal classroom experience in either elementary or secondary education, especially in recent years.

On the other hand, some scholars believe teaching is and will always be an art form. The very nature of teaching weaves a narrative beyond a lesson plan to create learning for both teachers and students. Every day that a teacher enters a classroom, they bring a persona, a soul, life experiences, knowledge, and a vivid display of how to transmit any knowledge students desire to know. The art of teaching encompasses a teaching philosophy, interactions with students, and complex elements infused from the design of a lesson — components of this nature that are not measured, quantified, or qualified. Through the art of teaching, one orchestrates the most dynamic components of teaching and learning, creating an atmosphere filled with color and expression, and thus, breathlessly waiting to return and complete a masterpiece each day.

John Dewey described teachers as composers, social engineers, and of course, artists (Lord, 2007). Teachers who ascribe to the belief that teaching is an art form create an environment to invite intellectual curiosity and cultivate the art of debate and dialogue, free expressions of knowledge that support learning beyond the obvious. The art of teaching creates pathways beyond classrooms so that endless ribbons of learning transfer from teachers to students. Learning must take place beyond guided theory and data. Learning must be crafted by an artist so that students embody and experience their own intellectual and creative understanding of knowledge in and outside the classroom.

Excellence in Teaching

Research that focuses on instruction intertwines with learning theories, but theories about learning are different from theories of teaching (Yamamoto, 1969). Deciding if an individual possesses the best teacher qualities, school districts assess teacher quality with variables such as grade point averages (GPA), SAT/ACT assessment test scores, and overall educational background. According to Sherman et al., 1987, teacher effectiveness is more accurately assessed by teacher actions and student scores on standardized tests. Definitions of excellent teaching can be complicated, but the following are components (Sherman et al., 1987):

- Excellent teaching is the application of the proper instructional treatments to identified academic problems.
- Excellent teaching is sequential, consistent, highly organized, prepared, and well planned.
- Excellent teaching is controlling and managing the classroom and class time to create a safe and learning-oriented environment.
- Excellent teaching is communicative, exemplifying excellent presentation and demonstration skills.
- Excellent teaching is setting and communicating elevated expectations for all students.
- Excellent teaching is skilled questions, utilizing a variety of cognitive levels, and reacting to and teaching from student responses.
- Excellent teaching is reflective and flexible, constantly changing and adapting to new contexts and learners. Excellent teaching is highly interactive and cooperative, building a community of learners working toward common purposes through caring and trusting relationships.
- Excellent teaching is building connections between- and within- subjects, contexts, and experiences.
- Excellent teaching is inclusive of multiple perspectives and empowering diverse populations and cultures.
- Excellent teaching is enthusiastic and expressive of excitement about the content.
- Excellent teaching embodies moral and ethical action and decision- making.

In the end, the correct understanding of teaching depends on conceptualizing teaching as a science (experimental sciences) and art, given that both present different analytical outcomes. Studying teaching as a science or art follows the need to identify what excellent teaching looks like in education and questioning how excellent teaching supports intended goals or outcomes established by educational initiatives. If intended outcomes are transmissions of academic content from teacher to student, then excellent teaching is communicative, requires excellent presentations, and demonstration skills (Jackson, 1986). On the other hand, if excellent teaching is based on highly interactive, cooperative environments, and building a community of learners working toward common purposes through caring and trusting relationships, according to Brazilian educator Paulo Freire, then excellence in teaching creates a dialogue of equals who work toward common goals (Freire, 2011).

Some scholars suggest that sufficient influences on learning are direct influences, such as the number of times teachers engage on a topic and the quality of social interactions between teachers and students. Less focus on indirect influences such as policies adopted by school districts, states, or other organizational features, including site-based management, is needed to achieve academic success for students (Wang et al., 2018). Further, if significant and direct influences on learning include student aptitude, classroom instruction, and climate, context, and program design, then teacher excellence must embrace reciprocal teaching and cognitive skills instruction (Wang et al., 2018).

More compelling than the ability to determine teacher excellent is determining where the excellent teachers are likely to work. According to Dreeben (1987), reading outcomes for over 300 first-graders were not based on the student's socioeconomic status or race, but the quality of instruction from teachers; level of learning connects to quality instruction. The study concluded that, on average, the quality of instruction for Black students was lower than the quality white students received. The National Assessment of Educational Progress (NAEP) also documented a direct correlation between qualified teachers and reading achievement. Both studies speak to unequal distribution of teacher excellence, especially for students of color who are more likely to encounter inadequate, inexperienced, and less-qualified educators. Research indicates that unqualified and underprepared educators are disproportionately found in low-income school districts where they are instructing students of color, whereas excellence in teaching occurs in more desirable schools.

Who Will Teach Students of Color

Whether evaluating education as a science or an art, students of color are far more likely to experience teaching environments controlled by research-based data. The same data are used to judge their achievement outcomes, even though students of color are far less likely to encounter experienced teachers, seldom receive an abundance of educational resources that support their academic achievement, and are likely to encounter white teachers who approach the population with deficient thinking.

Teacher excellence, a highly debated topic, presents as the single most powerful impact on student achievement (Hattie, 2004). However, no consensus has been reached on what excellence in teaching involves and indeed such excellence does not exist for most students in public schools—students of color. An intricate part of their journey is tied to teacher quality, but the best teachers leave the classroom for administrative positions (an increase in salary) or have multiple options to choose from.

Teachers with less experience or poor teaching ability contribute to weaker performance by students in high-poverty and resegregated schools. Schools with high concentrations of poor and low-achieving students can neither attract nor retain teachers, especially highly skilled educators. According to Boyd et al., 2011, teachers tend to favor wealthy school districts that offer more commitment to academic success, parental involvement, and high student achievement levels. However, school quality, consistency of teacher quality, and the quality of instruction are attributes that all schools must offer to eradicate educational inequality.

At the same time, schools are designed to prepare students for successful entry into the labor market (Hanushek & Somers, 2001), and we assume that advancing one's education level increases wealth. Despite this, neither component eliminates the widening income distribution between whites and Blacks, and the stagnating wages of Black workers. In essence, economic inequalities eliminate successful entry into the labor market, disqualify multiple levels of educational attainment for Blacks, and allow the wealth gap between whites and Blacks to expand. This scenario indicates that the future of work for students of color is challenged by the influences of systematic racism.

Students of color in public schools are marginalized, and their educational journey suppressed by data even though the quality of their school environment can remove income inequality, wage disparities, and provide skills for life-sustaining employment related to the future of work. However, these indispensable elements elude students of color who are forced to intentionally attend resegregated schools and live in low-income and poverty enclaves.

Improving the quality of schools for low-income children must be consciously deliberate otherwise technological and automation innovations will permanently remove them from participating in a global economy. The nature of systemic racism allows generations of students to consistently encounter economic and social inequalities produced by globalization, the future of work, and a wealth gap. In the end, both students of color and their families are permanently trapped with no options for economic stability. Is it no wonder that prison offers three meals a day, cable television, and health care?

Choosing to teach requires that the best teachers in America interact with over 24 million children who attend high-poverty schools. In the 2015-16 school year, 40 percent of public school students in cities attended high-poverty schools, 20 percent in town schools, 18 percent in suburban schools, and 15 percent in rural schools (Concentration of Public School Students Eligible for Free or Reduced- Price Lunch, 2018). This option is not likely to occur given the massive number of teachers who are retiring, and their replacements do not exist. Without question, there are teachers available to fill vacancies in public schools, and they are likely to choose predominately white school districts. The massive exit of Black Career Educators and other teachers of color will leave low-income and resegregated school districts with a large number of teacher vacancies, advance the wealth gap between whites and people of color, and further destroy equality in education for the majority population in public schools—children of color.

Reasons to Teach

As a teacher, I appreciate each student who enters the classroom. However, the ability to teach and transfer knowledge is not dependent on innate qualities, loving students, and showing a secure emotional attachment toward students. Some students love and appreciate their teachers regardless of any attempts by a teacher to practice emotional detachment. Remember, not all teaching experiences are in Mr. Roger's neighborhood. Teaching requires wisdom, understanding of multiple cultures, and a transfer of values to students that apply to a student's life. Teaching requires an array of skills and knowledge in multiple academic disciplines while understanding a school community, and the socioeconomic and political concerns. Teachers who do not teach perfect populations of students know that understanding a student's reality is essential to positive educational outcomes.

There are benefits when teachers form positive bonds with students, and outcomes are both academically and socially productive. According to Gallagher (2017), there is extensive research at the elementary level but less research at the middle and high school levels about the positive effects of teacher and student relationships. Collectively, we know student motivation in school is linked to positive encounters with educators who play a significant role in a student's academic achievements by establishing positive, caring, and supportive relationships. Furthermore, while research often depicts a focus on promoting the health and well-being of students, less emphasis is placed on the emotional health of teachers. Very few school environments resemble Sesame Street, and even ideal school environments are vulnerable to stress and violence, especially gun violence.

After 35 years, I cannot imagine another career choice. My joy of teaching is insurmountable, and opportunities aligned with my teaching career are cherished. The more I taught, the more I created a path to my zenith, a place where I caught the wind. My return to the classroom each fall included every idea and inspiration collected during summers—inspirations and ideas to share and explore with individuals who were my replacement on the planet.

Teachers create memories, instill a value for knowledge, share advice, and influence an individual's future and career choice. A teacher transfers values, culture, and a road map to the next journey outside their classroom. We are only one steppingstone in our students' journeys but a small part of their pathway through life.

When Black Career Educators Chose to Teach

As a Black Career Educator, my career is not a single journey. There are thousands of Black Career Educators, and our career journeys must be written and framed—framed in the context of America's structural racism that systemically removed, disenfranchised, and marginalized our professional journeys. The mere presence of Black educators created a violent response enforced by laws and policies to imply that we were unsuitable, unlicensed, inexperienced, and by no means could be placed in a classroom with white students, for we were barely qualified to instruct Black children. Society was not interested in our teaching philosophy or values and beliefs about the purpose of education. Instead, society questioned our dedication, qualifications, and distorted perceptions about our professionalism.

With teaching comes an emotional journey that is seldom shared, and I am not sure why we hold components of our emotional journey in our souls. With teaching comes joys of student success and sorrows of their disappointments. With teaching comes good years and not so good years, wondering if you can continue or want to continue to be a teacher.

Still, we do more than teaching. We raise individuals. We feed individuals. We wipe away tears, and we find ways to restore happiness. When others ran away, we stayed, endured, and created a path for success. We endured the threats, the challenges, and the disappointments. When others ran away, we stayed to heal the wounds inflicted by the luck of the draw, and we believed that Black children did not ask to come into the world, but someone had to provide care, and where a child grows, the environment defines their life experiences. Besides, if you are a Black Career Educator, you taught amid society trying to subvert your professional career. Sadly, we cannot stay forever and challenge inequalities; only society can destroy inequalities.

2 BLACK EDUCATORS BEFORE, DURING, AND AFTER BROWN

Before Brown

The Greek historian Diodorus Siculus stated that intelligence and learning came from Egypt, and Egyptian priests recorded the visits of Plato, Pythagoras of Samos, Eudoxus, and others who also believed the center of knowledge existed in Egypt. Greek philosophers studied philosophy and medicine for decades in Egypt before philosophy existed during the Greek Golden Era, thus proving that philosophy existed in Africa long before there were Greek philosophers (Asante, 2000).

So often, the nature and reality of knowledge is a challenge for humans. Moreover, general perceptions throughout history do not place thinkers and lovers of knowledge from the continent of Africa, even though customs, teachings, art, and mathematics belong to Africans. When this undisputed evidence emerges, suddenly, Egyptians are not Africans. However, the scholarly works of Professor Cheeks Anta Diop and, more recently, DNA testing confirms that Egyptians were not only Africans but Black Africans (Kishinev, 1970). Before DNA confirmation, scholars argued that racial prejudice had no role in ancient society. The matter of Black or Egyptian was artificial (Yurco, 1989). The color of skin, black or brown, did not symbolize inferiority or a barrier in society (Snowden, 1983). The ancient Egyptian population, over millennia intermingled with multiple indigenous people (Kelly, 1991).

Historically, the gathering and disbursement of knowledge throughout the continent of Africa were endless. The Ancient Empire of Ghana (existed c. 750- 1076) stood as an empire rich in culture, wealth, and a center of education. Later annexed by Mali, the largest empire in West Africa (founded in 1235 CE), Mali evolved as another center of knowledge.

In Mali, Sankore University operated with fully staffed educators. The most extensive collections of books, in both Africa and the world, were found at the university. With over 1,000,000 manuscripts on subjects from medicine to astronomy, over 25,000 students attended the university, and in the city of Timbuktu, there were schools, institutions, and the earliest university campuses (Magirosa, 2014). The history of sharing knowledge and teaching was a woven entity throughout the continent of Africa, where scholars and educators traveled freely as global educators. Sadly, the arrival of Europeans onto African soil resulted in burning down buildings, looting, and destroying the wealth of architecture, history, and prosperity.

Even at the dawn of the transatlantic slave trade, Africa represented diversity, ancient cultures, and more than 800 languages. These were cultures influenced by Arab North Africans, consisting of cosmopolitan cities, and large kingdoms such as Mali, Songhay, and Benin (African Immigration, 2019). By the sixteenth century, the capital of Benin was one of the largest cities in the world. All of this indicates that expansive civilizations existed on the continent of Africa before the arrival of Europeans.

Africans in North America

Africans were not only global educators, but global explorers as well. There are several examples of African scholars arriving in North America, and with their arrival came the transfer of knowledge. As early as the 1500s, Africans traveled across Mexico, Peru, and Ecuador, and they saw the Pacific Ocean alongside Vasco Nunez de Balboa (African Immigration, 2019). The great African explorer, Estevanico, explored the Southwestern part of the United States with Francisco Vazquez de Coronado. Estevanico, a polyglot, met with Native American tribes, and learned to communicate with them in their native languages (African Immigration, 2019).

Africans came to Florida in the late 1500s, and by the 1700s, freed slaves constructed the Castillo de San Marcos in St. Augustine, Florida. In 1738, free Blacks built the first Black settlement in America called Fort Mose, which consisted of churches and shops (Deagan & MacMahon, 1995). Artifacts from the site, which is a National Historic Landmark on the Florida Black Heritage Trail, indicate a rich culture and a society of traditions that demonstrate the transfer of knowledge, skills, and teachings from scholars. Collectively, Africans arrived in North America and later the United States, with cognitive wealth.

Early Education of Blacks

Blacks were prohibited by law to learn how to read and write during the America slave experience. Slave owners fearing literacy would prove a major threat to the slave experience. Minor exceptions existed where Black children attended school in the late 1600s and early 1700s, but this was not a norm for Black children, whether free or slaves. Interesting to note, John Chavis, the first Black American to receive a college education in the United States, graduated from what is now Washington and Lee University in 1799. Imagine if most Blacks living in America had that opportunity without the influence of structural racism.

Early opportunities to educate Black children in the United States challenged the first Black educators who participated in this extraordinary web of complexities. They were legends who are seldom mentioned, if ever, in textbooks or during Black History Month celebrations. They are individuals lost in the untold history of Blacks in America.

By the late 1700s, Black preachers were instrumental in advancing literacy. Their efforts in Pennsylvania, Louisiana, and New York were evident in schools for free Blacks, which included Black educators. Nevertheless, not all Black educators were in a classroom.

Phillis Wheatley (1753-1784), born in Senegal/Gambia (West Africa), published the first book of poetry written by a Black female. Quobna Ottobah Cugoano (born in 1757 in present-day Ghana), an African critic of the Transatlantic Slave Trade, published *Thoughts and Sentiments on the Evil and Wicked Traffic of the Slavery and Commerce of the Human Species*, in 1787. Born in 1745, Olaudah Equiano (Gustavus Vassa) was a seaman and merchant who wrote an autobiography about slavery in 1789. He was the son of a chief in West Africa (Igbo) before he was kidnapped and sold into slavery. Born in 1788, Mary Prince presented a petition to the British Parliament on anti-slavery and published an autobiography. While limited, this list of individuals indicates the beginning of the African diaspora and contributions to global knowledge during the 1700s.

From the seventeenth century to the eighteenth century, individuals of African descent continued to advance global knowledge. Benjamin Banneker, born in 1731, was a prominent eighteenth-century Black scholar who was taught reading and religion by his grandmother, continued his education in a one-room Quaker school, and was self-educated and a voracious reader. During his lifetime, Banneker mastered mathematics, astronomy, was an essayist, and pamphleteer. Banneker shared his knowledge and continued to publish annually until 1797.

In 1798, more schools for colored children opened in Boston, New York City, and Philadelphia. The educators were from philanthropic and voluntary organizations that educated free Blacks (Frazier, 1957). The American Missionary Association (AMA) provided educators who were free women of color from the North but educated in England. AMA continued to open schools in Virginia, North Carolina, and South Carolina (Frazier, 1957), thus providing more opportunities for free Blacks to forward their education and skills.

In Virginia, free individuals established the first Black secondary school in the state and continued to teach free individuals. Between 1861 and the end of Reconstruction, Black educators represented more than one-third of the educators teaching in Virginia's first Black schools. Black educators were committed and instructed Black students long after white teachers left schools established by the Freedmen's Bureau.

Throughout the South, Black educators and freed Blacks continued to initiate educational opportunities for southern Blacks (Butchart, 2017c). Whether they arrived as free Africans or were forced into slavery, Blacks brought a wealth of erudition, skills, and a passion for learning. They brought a voice. They translated their inward knowledge into words that exist today — proving that one cannot take away the internal workings of the mind and the generational passing of culture, customs, and teachings.

Education During Slavery

The political power of literacy was motivation for Blacks before and after the American Civil War of 1861-1865. During slavery, there were enormous efforts by both slaves and freed individuals to obtain an education in the United States. According to Litwack (1998), Blacks knew that knowledge meant independence, free thoughts, and that power, influence, and wealth linked to literacy.

Before Nat Turner's 1831 rebellion, slave owners feared literacy would empower slaves to rebel. If Blacks remained illiterate, they remained oppressed by a tool that influenced their economic, social, and political status in the United States. All decisions to prohibit education for Black slaves served the needs of plantation owners who offered a variety of opinions on the matter. The education of Blacks, in general, was controlled by individuals who would not economically benefit from providing education to slaves. As Carter G. Woodson so eloquently stated in *The Mis-Education of the Negro* (1933), Blacks were never educated, only informed about the world, and their education subjected to the will of others.

Regardless of the overall sentiment from plantation owners, some educators desired to educate Black children before the end of the Civil War. A white Union army chaplain, Vincent Colyer, taught escaped slaves and established the first school for freed individuals in North Carolina on Roanoke Island in 1863. Another white soldier taught and opened a school in New Bern, North Carolina (Butchart, 2010a). At the same time, the desire to educate freed individuals and slaves did not fall solely into the hands of whites. Catherine Williams Ferguson, born into slavery in 1779, could not read but worked relentlessly in New York City's lower Manhattan, helping both Black and white destitute children. By 1814, she established the Murray Street Sabbath School, and by 1818 records indicated the school had 88 students. A total of 26 students were Black, and 62 were white. Working with Rev. John Mitchell Mason, who assisted with finding educators to teach school subjects, Ferguson supported the school with money she earned, especially as a caterer (Haskins et al., 2002).

Black Career Educator Charlotte Forten, a freeborn woman, instructed Black children and adults in the South Carolina sea islands in 1862, one of the first schools built by the Freedmen's Bureau. The Atlantic Monthly published her teaching experiences in 1864. According to Ms. Forten, "I never before saw children so eager to learn," she remarks, "although I had had several years' experience in New England schools."

Charles L. Reason (1818-1893), a child prodigy in mathematics, later studied at the McGrawville College, and in 1849 became the first Black university professor. However, his desire to teach started at the African Free School in New York City when he was 14 years old. Interesting to note, even though female students attended the African Free School, there is no mention of female educators at the school (New York African Free School Collection, 2019).

Black Career Educator Mary Jane Patterson graduated from Oberlin College in 1862. Patterson was the first Black woman to receive a college education, and she served as the first Black principal of Preparatory High School for Negroes (later named Paul Dunbar High School) in Washington, DC, in 1871 (Terrell, 1917). Patterson's sisters Chanie and Emeline, were graduates of Oberlin College and Black Career Educators as well.

Holistically, most educators of Blacks before the Civil War were clergymen (Woodson, 1915). Even German Protestants and Spanish and French Christians chose to educate Black slaves. Later, the English with the help of The Society for the Propagation of the Gospel in Foreign Parts, and Quakers in Northern parts of the United States provided a strong influence on the need to educate Blacks (Woodson, 1915).

This book provides a minimal account of individuals and organizations working to educate both freed individuals and slaves before the Civil War. However, the desire to seek knowledge, share knowledge, develop ventures to knowledge, and eradicate illiteracy, continued even though challenged by structural racism.

Before Brown and After the Civil War

Before 1860, public schools in the South, where most Blacks lived, were rudimentary, and after the Civil War, southern states created a dual educational system based on race (Smithsonian, 2019). Nevertheless, there was a sense of obligation in Black communities by teachers and parents to educate Blacks, build schools, and maintain schools that embodied their values. Surprisingly, after the Civil War and during Reconstruction (1865-1877), more freed persons attended school, even more so than whites (Fairclough, 2007).

For Blacks living in the South, education became a priority and symbolized respect, a good life, and advantages in society. However, the quality of schools varied from state to state in the South, and the desire for education demanded that Blacks create their schools in abandoned cabins and buildings, and Black churches. By 1868, most educators, especially in rural areas, were Black educators. Northern educators or northern evangelicals, clergymen, and social workers traveled to the South in the 1870s but lived in urban areas and naturally, did not teach the 90 percent of Blacks living in rural areas (Fairclough, 2007).

While northern missionaries arrived in the South soon after the start of the Civil War, several missionaries remained after the war, especially Methodists from the African Methodist Episcopal Church and the African Methodist Episcopal Zion Church. James Walker Hood, an African Methodist Episcopal Zion Church bishop, arrived from Connecticut and established over 350 churches in North Carolina, South Carolina, and Virginia. Each church built a school, and several started newspapers (Inge, 2019).

Southern Blacks received support from the Freedmen's Bureau (established in 1865). However, the Bureau's support offered limited resources and failed to meet the tremendous requirements needed to educate Blacks in the South. By the summer of 1872, Congress responded to pressure from white Southerners and dismantled the Freedmen's Bureau. Still, Black communities, often desperately poor, created resources to establish and maintain schools.

Black parents in northern cities were demanding that their children attend public schools as early as the 1840s. In Boston, Benjamin Roberts organized a legal campaign to enroll his daughter (Sarah) in a white school. The lawsuit was heard by the

Massachusetts Supreme Court, which ruled that local elected officials had the authority to control local schools and that separate schools did not violate Black students' rights. The ruling from this case was used repeatedly to support segregation in public schools. However, Roberts retained two attorneys, Charles Sumner (abolitionist and later a United States Senator) and Robert Morris, a Black abolitionist lawyer from Boston. In April 1850, the Supreme Judicial Court ruled that the school committee could establish education policy and that there was no constitutional reason for abolishing Black schools, though segregated (Johnson, 1992). Black parents in Boston did not accept the ruling and organized school boycotts and statewide protests. By 1855, the Massachusetts legislature passed the first law in the United States that prohibited school segregation.

Attending a public school after the Civil War was challenging, regardless of where Blacks lived. By the 1870s, Jim Crow laws consumed public education and fiercely enforced racial segregation, especially in southern states. In northern states, housing and racial segregation enforced segregation in public schools, and naturally controlled which public schools Black students could attend. The most defining resistance arrived in 1896 with the Supreme Court decision, *Plessy v. Ferguson*, which established separate public schools for Black and white students. Combined with no attempt to fully finance Black schools, structural racism dismantled public education for Blacks in America.

Training Black Career Educators

Whether training to become an educator or finding dynamic ways to ensure that Black children and children of color received an education, numerous individuals began their professional careers as educators. They were individuals who stepped outside of the prescribed role intended for Blacks and paved their destiny.

In the mid-1800s, Blacks were unlikely to be aware of or believe that Hawaii, not a state until 1959, offered opportunities outside of structural racism. T. McCants Stewart, a freedman, born in Charleston, South Carolina in 1852, attended Howard University in Washington, DC, and later the University of South Carolina at Columbia to receive a law degree in 1875. He practiced law in Orangeburg, South Carolina, before sailing to Hawaii in 1898. His trip to Hawaii provided an opportunity for Stewart's daughter, Carlotta Stewart. Carlotta completed her college education in Hawaii and pursued a career as a teacher and principal in Hawaii. Carlotta died in 1952 (Broussard, 2007).

St. Augustine's Normal School and Collegiate Institute in Raleigh, North Carolina, was chartered in 1867 to instruct future Black educators. The school officially opened in 1868 and provided education in both the primary and high school grades.

One of the most distinguished graduates was born a slave in 1858. Dr. Anna Julia Haywood Cooper attended St. Augustine starting in 1868. She tutored and became an instructor at St. Augustine before graduating from Oberlin College in 1884. Dr. Cooper taught at Wilberforce College and later taught and was principal of M Street High School in Washington, DC (now known as Paul Dunbar High School). She completed her doctoral degree in France at the University of Paris-Sorbonne in 1925 (North Carolina Department of Cultural Resources, 2018).

Born in Victoria, British Columbia, Canada, in 1862, Ida Gibbs Hunt graduated from Oberlin College in 1884. She taught Latin and mathematics at Florida Agricultural and Mechanical in Tallahassee, Florida, and later taught at the M Street High School in Washington, DC.

In 1874, the father of a college graduate, Mary Jane Wilson, constructed a school for his daughter in their backyard. At times, she taught as many as 75 students, and several became educators (Litwack, 1998).

All these accounts tell a story, though extremely brief as there are so many pioneer Black Career Educators waiting to be illustrated on white pages and in black ink. Black Career Educators organized efforts to educate Black students after the Civil War and their relentless and creative approaches to ensure that Blacks received an education were endless. Individuals who had opportunities to advance their education shared their awareness, and never regretted their participation in the struggle against racism.

Black Career Educators, North and South

Southern rural communities were the most challenging for Black Career Educators. They received meager salaries, and sometimes no salary was offered. In some communities, it took Black parents 2 or 3 months to earn a teacher's monthly salary. Other Black rural communities afforded room and board for a monthly salary (Litwack (1998).

The inferior quality of public schools in Daytona Beach, Florida, inspired Mary McLeod Bethune to open the Daytona Normal and Industrial Institute for Negro Girls in 1904. From only five students, she advanced the school enrollment to more than 250 students and served as the Institute's president. In 1923, she combined the school with the Cookman Institute for Men, later known as Bethune-Cookman College (Mary McLeod Bethune, 2019).

Dr. John Robert Edward Lee (1864-1944), founder of the American Educators Association, was born into slavery in Seguin, Texas, and graduated from Bishop

College in 1889 with a degree in elementary and secondary education. After several teaching experiences, he moved to Palestine, Texas, to be a principal of a two-teacher school. As dean and professor at Bishop College, he taught Latin, mathematics, and history. Lee was awarded a Doctor of Laws from for his contributions to Black education. Later, as the president of Florida Agricultural and Mechanical University (FAMU) in 1924, he received accreditation for the university and increased salaries for educators and administrators (Neyland 1962).

In 1904, Lee founded the National Association of Educators in Colored Schools, which provided a platform for Black Career Educators. Black educators in both the middle atlantic and southern states were members (14 state associations and membership of over 12,000) who received the quarterly publication of The American Educators Association Bulletin (Martin, 1950). The name of the organization changed in 1937 to the American Teachers Association (ATA), but the mission remained the same.

Black Career Educators in southern communities were relentless, creative, and phenomenal. They wrote curricula, designed model academic programs, and established institutions of higher education. Each of their accomplishments advanced the well-being of Black students and members of the Black community. Imagine what they would have accomplished without the restrictions of racist policies and laws.

In northern cities during the post-Civil War period, unwritten rules controlled segregated schools and, thus, the education of Black children. Nevertheless, the structure of society did not control Octavius Valentine Catto. Catto grew up in Philadelphia, attended elite city grammar schools, the Academy in Allentown in New Jersey, and finally, the Institute for Colored Youth in Philadelphia, PA (later Cheyney University). The Institute provided Black students a free college-level education and focused on preparing students to become educators. Catto graduated in 1858 as valedictorian, started teaching at the Institute, and later served as an assistant principal (Biddle & Dubin, 2010).

Like so many Black Career Educators, Catto was an activist who worked to remove segregation and discrimination in Philadelphia's transportation, sports, politics, and society. Sadly, one year after the Fifteenth Amendment to the U.S. Constitution restored voting rights to Blacks, on Election Day in 1871, Catto died on the streets of Philadelphia for his activism (Biddle & Dubin, 2010). The murder of Catto did not stand as a deterrent. Instead, Black Career Educators responded as if activism was a professional requirement. Educators joined national organizations and continued their activism for equality in education at both the local and national level.

Black Career Educators outside of the classroom acquired a social role, and for so many Black communities, they were role models, individuals with scholarly and intellectual abilities who articulated how public schools systemically underdeveloped educational opportunities for Black students. Their journeys were laced with academic preparation, pedagogical training, discrimination, and segregation—ultimately landing them in positions that left them powerless, neglected, and expecting to fail. Despite these obstacles, the challenge, while daunting, did not discourage Black Career Educators, who continued to instruct Black students, who became principals, and college presidents—all positions that advanced opportunities for Black students and strengthened Black communities.

Neither slaves nor free individuals misconstrued the power of literacy and knowledge. This consistent pursuit of education is not a transformative power cultivated by the arrival of Africans in North America, but merely an innate quality shared by ancestors from Africa. This type of innate quality for the pursuit of educating Blacks in America was braided with activism. Activism in the Black community led by Black Career Educators.

Harlem Educators

As Blacks migrated to northern cities, the number of Black professionals living in northern cities increased, especially during the 1920s. The migration, driven by the impact of southern Jim Crow laws, lynching violence, unemployment, and a desire for better public schools for Black students, increased the population of Blacks in northern cities. As more Blacks moved to New York City, especially Harlem, by the 1930s, 70 percent of the population in Harlem was Black (Gotham Gazette, 2008). Naturally, this population dynamic increased the number of Black children attending public schools in Harlem.

New York law prohibited public school segregation, and Harlem's schools contained both Black and white students in the 1920s. However, housing patterns created by de facto segregation increased the probability of all Black neighborhoods and all-Black schools. Even though the student population was entirely Black, the teaching population remained overwhelmingly white. By 1928, of the 500 teachers who taught in Harlem's eight public schools, only 100 were Black, and that proportion of Black educators was higher than other northern cities (Robertson et al., 2013).

The migration to Harlem seemed ambitious and opened the possibility for better public school opportunities. However, the decrease in the number of white students attending Harlem schools, increasing white teacher turnover, and changes in the curriculum in Harlem's schools in response to the increasing number of Black students was problematic for Black parents (Robertson et al., 2013).

Changes in the curriculum, adjusted by New York City's white administrators, meant Black males received more vocational training courses (low-skilled machinery and service industry etiquette) instead of academic courses. Black girls were directed toward dressmaking and domestic courses instead of academic courses. If Black students attended high school, they left Harlem to attend schools in other communities. In 1926, according to one study, only 507 Black students attended high school in New York City (Robertson et al., 2013). By the 1930s, public schools in Harlem were over capacity, and the Great Depression only decreased funding for public schools and caused schools in Harlem to deteriorate.

The role of Black Career Educators in Harlem demanded both teaching and social activism. According to Johnson (2004), Lucile Spence, Gertrude Elise McDougald Ayer, and Layla Lane spent over 40 years as social reformers, union organizers, civil rights leaders, and educators in Harlem. Each educator worked to eradicate social and economic inequalities in Harlem's Black community, especially before and after the Harlem Riot in 1935. The riot centered around an incident at the S. H. Kress dime store and resulted in over 100 individuals being arrested and injured, and three individuals dying, all of them Black.

In response to the Harlem Riot, Mayor La Guardia established the Harlem Commission to study catalysts for the riot. Harlem educators testified and described the unsanitary and dilapidated school buildings, outdated curriculums, prejudice presented by white educators, and the lack of social and psychological services. In addition to Harlem educators testifying, Black residents of Harlem described incidents of employment discrimination, police brutality, and substandard schools. The complete details of the report appeared in The Amsterdam News on July 18, 1936.

Black Career Educators were not the majority population in New York City public schools, but they were a voice against structural racism in Harlem. By 1936, Black educators were estimated to represent only 2 to 3 percent (800 educators) of the teaching population (Tyack, 1974). In the 1940s, according to the Educators Union of New York City, Black Career Educators were assigned to Black neighborhood schools in the boroughs and communities of the southeast Bronx, Harlem in Manhattan, and Bedford-Stuyvesant in Brooklyn. They were likely to teach over 33,000 school-age children living in Harlem by the 1940s (Ment, 1983). Lucile Spence (1899-1975) was born in South Carolina. After moving to New York City, she attended Wadleigh High School, located at 215 West 114th Street, an all-girls high school in Harlem, founded in 1902. After graduating cum laude in 1923 from Hunter College in New York City, she obtained a masters from Columbia University in 1926 and joined Phi Beta Kappa

(Hunter College Archives, 1923). Spence taught biology at Wadleigh High School in 1926 and worked diligently for the Educators Union of New York City (later known as Educators Union), an organization formed in 1916 with 600 members. The Educators Union focused on espousing equal educational opportunities, academic freedom, progressive education, and presenting Black life and history in public schools (Johnson, 2002). Spence worked as an activist well into the 1940s as a speaker for the Educators Union. She chaired a panel with a future *Brown* litigator and U.S. Supreme Court Justice, Thurgood Marshall, for equal educational opportunities and wrote a series of articles supporting school integration (Johnson, 2002). Spence remained in Harlem until her death.

Gertrude Elise Johnson McDougald Ayer (often referred to as Elise McDougald Ayer) was born in New York City, the daughter of Dr. Peter A. Johnson. Dr. Johnson, one of the first Black physicians to practice in New York City, was a founder of the National Urban League. Ayer did not receive a bachelor's degree, although she completed coursework at Hunter College, Columbia University, and New York City College. Ayer started a teaching career in 1905 in lower Manhattan and later worked as a vocational counselor. By 1935, she received a temporary appointment as principal of PS 24 on Staten Island, a community experiencing high unemployment during the Great Depression. Ayer's effective social activism and testifying implemented child- centered progressive education that emphasized an intercultural curriculum. The new curriculum included experiential learning, self-directed projects, interdisciplinary courses, and democratic living. Ayer retired in 1954 but remained a social activist and writer.

Layla Lane, a native of Marietta, Georgia and daughter of Reverend Calvin Lane and Alice Clark Lane, followed in her mother's footsteps as an educator. Born in 1893, Lane's family left Georgia fearing her father would be lynched. The family settled in Knoxville, Tennessee and later moved to Vineland, New Jersey. Lane, the first Black graduate of Vineland High School, graduated from Howard University in 1916 and received her master's degree from Columbia University in New York City. She started her teaching career as a high school teacher in New York City (Layle Lane, 2017).

An activist throughout her life, Lane participated in protests, joined the Teachers Union and Teachers Guild, where she served on the executive board. Lane's leadership roles in education continued when elected the first Black female to serve as vice president for the American Federation of Teachers (United Federation of Teachers, 2017).

Lane ran for public office (Congress) on the Socialist Party ticket three times, served on the National Committee for Rural Schools, and in 1941 organized the March on Washington for Jobs and Freedom. With her own money, Lane purchased a farm in

Pennsylvania and established a summer camp for impoverished Black children from inner-city communities. She died in 1976 in Cuernavaca, Mexico (Schierenbeck, 2017).

Ayers, Spence, and Lane had spectacular careers and represented the lives, stories, and journeys of Black Career Educators. These educators were more than educators in their community, they were planners, organizers, orators, and the 'first' in many aspects. They were Black Career Educators that changed lives, communities, and history.

Southern Communities After the Civil War

In the South, public schools for Blacks were provocative. Few Black children remained in school beyond primary grades, and they were likely to attend inferior schools. The schools were devoid of supplies, books, and furniture. However, Black Career Educators in these communities were extraordinarily talented and innovative. So often, they created alternative essentials they needed for teaching, and despite inadequate supplies, facilities, and salaries, a steady expansion in the number of Black educators occurred in southern cities.

As early as 1869, southern Blacks were a majority in the teaching force, especially in primary schools. By the early twentieth century, Black Career Educators outnumbered all educators in post-primary schools. This expansion increased the number of Black women entering the teaching profession as well. In North Carolina, Black female and male public school educators were almost equal in number by 1902.

The education level of Black educators in the Jim Crow south faced challenges when Horace Mann Bond administered the Stanford Achievement Test to Black educators in Alabama in 1931. Bond indicated that Black educators barely scored above the 8th grade level (Irons, 2004). The irony is that very few southern communities offered education beyond the elementary level, especially for Blacks. There were very few segregated high schools for Blacks in the South. Black students who were fortunate enough to attend high school paid tuition. For Black rural families, affording the cost to educate their children beyond elementary grades meant great financial sacrifice. Thus, everyone with any desire to teach, regardless of their education level, were called upon to assist. While Bond portrays Black educators as poorly educated, Black Career Educators in other southern states often exceeded an 8th-grade education and the education level of white teachers.

Former teacher Louise Metoyer Boise attended public schools in New Orleans during the 1920s and 1930s. According to Boise, "I didn't feel I was getting an inferior education...in fact, I am sure I had very good educators" (Fairclough, 2002). Even in the crude, two-room schoolhouse which she attended in rural North Carolina, Mildred

Oakley Page, a retired Black Career Educator, insisted, "anyone who wanted to learn could learn" (Fairclough, 2002).

Regardless of standardized test results, Black educators in the South were very caring individuals and viewed themselves as professionals trained to instruct Black children. In many communities, as expected, Black Career Educators did more than teaching. They provided order, prevailed, demanded respect, and received it from parents and students. Education was a collective responsibility in the Black community, and educators held a prestigious position (Fairclough, 2002).

Solidifying Structural Racism in the South

The United States Declaration of Independence written 1776 states that "all men are created equal." However, the institution of slavery did not consider this component and not until after the Civil War, and later the Thirteenth Amendment (1865) to the Constitution of the United States did the United States revisit equality. By 1868, the Constitution's Fourteenth Amendment provides additional legal rights for freed persons by indicating "due process of law" and "equal protection of the law." Finally, the Constitution's Fifteenth Amendment (1870) prohibited states from denying freed persons the right to vote due to race. Regardless of progress, several southern states implemented policies (Jim Crow laws) that promoted segregation, especially in public schools. Interestingly, southern states did not create a segregated school system immediately after the Civil War, given the failure to establish public education before the Civil War. For example, in New Orleans, Louisiana, integrated public schools existed until 1877.

U.S. Supreme Court Justice Henry B. Brown cited cases between 1849 and 1880 in eight different states which established separate (segregated) public schools for Black students. According to Irons (2004), three assumptions came from these cases. First, judges had to defer to judgments of elected lawmakers and school officials, stating that segregation existed in the best interest of all children. Second, the Fourteenth Amendment's "equal protection of the laws" did not apply to education. Third, laws did not create, nor could they remove the prejudices of voters and parents. Thus, the cases gave precedent for the *Plessy v. Ferguson* decision, which settled as a landmark 1896 U.S. Supreme Court decision to uphold the constitutionality of racial segregation under the "separate but equal" doctrine. This decision solidified Jim Crow schools in the United States, especially in the South, where most Blacks lived in rural communities. Southern segregated schools for Blacks were also a reflection of the jobs available to Blacks, sharecropping, and domestic service. Both jobs required only basic literacy obtained in some of the most dilapidated schools one could imagine. Further, southern environments limited educational opportunities for Blacks by withdrawing school funds and firmly implementing virulent racism throughout southern society. Heading into the twentieth century, Black professionals, such as teachers, physicians, and ministers, comprised only 2 percent of the southern Black population, and the Great Depression only deepened the refusal to fund Black education in the South.

During Brown

Authors Anderson and Moss (1999) state that during the 1930s, donations from northern philanthropic groups to southern communities to support the education of Blacks were dangerous and came with limitations. Foundations were cautious and certainly needed approval from southern communities when forwarding support to Black communities for public schools. When approved, with the intention that Blacks needed education for productive participation in the southern economy, participating in the southern economic system did not necessarily benefit Blacks.

Dr. Carter G. Woodson wrote *The Mis-Education of the Negro* in 1933 and commented on how the miseducation of Black students crystallized into intellectual insecurities. Woodson believed Black students were denied race consciousness and needed education about Black history to build their legacy and social theory, which serves as an analytical tool for how societies change, especially as it relates to power, social structure, and race. By the 1930s, Jim Crow education rested on the will of others who had already enslaved the minds of Blacks.

In the 1930s, Black students attended Jim Crow schools in the North and South and often attended schools that lagged far behind white schools in facilities and teacher training (Irons, 2004). In the South, 3 million Black children lived in 17 states with segregated schools that stretched from Delaware to Texas. Very few finished grade schools or attended high school, and Black Career Educators seldom received academic support in professional development. As the Great Depression deepened, decreased financial support for public schools, at the expense of Black segregated schools, seemed evident in both southern and northern states. The allocation of school resources between white and Black schools was never equal, and the Great Depression expanded inequalities even though some Black communities in northern cities accepted segregated schools. Black parents viewed segregated school environments as opportunities to protect their children against white racist teachers.

From the 1940s to the 1960s, the national perspective toward ending school segregation, thanks to the efforts of the National Association for the Advancement of Colored People (NAACP), was promising. Together, the NAACP and the modern Civil Rights Movement established a goal to improve public school education for Blacks.

White educators and principals resisted any change. The nature of change implied that Black parents needed to change their cultural practices, which were responsible for the poor academic performance of Black students (Willie, Garibaldri & Reed, 1991). Even this outlook did not deter Black Career Educators who focused on increasing the number of Black students finishing high school. They advocated for a differentiated curriculum, changes in guidance programs that promoted high school completion, and adjustments in school calendars, given that Black and white students did not have the same school calendars. Black students attended school fewer days than white students with the expectation that Black students worked during harvest times, especially in rural areas. By advocating for high school completion, Black students would gain more significant economic advantages and racial consciousness (Juergensen, 2015).

Black Career Educators represented half of all Black professionals by the 1950s, but the push to desegregate public schools came with mixed emotions among Black educators and the Black community. The *Plessy v. Ferguson* decision supported structural racism and inequalities in public education in southern states with the use of Jim Crow laws. In the North, de facto segregation and racial isolation resulting from segregated housing gripped Black students attending public schools. Black Career Educators realized that fighting for change provided a critical turning point in public school education, and Black educators feared legal changes would jeopardize job security. As early as 1935, legal strategies designed by the NAACP convinced the Virginia Teachers Association to demand equal wages while establishing a fund to compensate teachers (plaintiffs) forced out of their teaching positions.

Black Career Educators in the North and South were active participants pushing to desegregate public schools. Throughout the struggle to desegregate public schools, their dedication to instructing Black students continued. According to Siddle-Walker (2000), during both pre- and post- desegregation, Black Career Educators retained lofty expectations for Black students and assumed Black students would receive a quality education.

After World War II, a post-war sentiment focused on education, especially educational equality in both public education and higher education for Blacks. However, even with the focus, the two most segregated components of American society were housing and education. Focus alone was not going to reconstruct racist housing and education practices.

In northern communities, segregated housing determined where Blacks should live and, thus, resulted in segregated schools. Segregated housing meant racial restrictions such as restrictive housing covenants, which clearly said Blacks were not allowed to live or purchase a home in specific communities. Both local and federal laws were written to protect white property values. However, Blacks continued to wage desegregation battles in northern cities from 1920 to the 1950s in both suburban areas and industrial towns (Jones, 2014).

Southern communities, where fears of educating Blacks wrapped around Jim Crow laws, provided resistance and allowed structural racism to prevail. Retaliation for speaking out against segregated schools in southern communities included burning down Black schools, firing Black teachers, evictions, harassment, and even refusing Black farmers bank credit or equipment to harvest crops, especially in rural southern communities. Black Career Educators feared joining and supporting the NAACP's efforts to desegregate Southern schools, but southern whites had no fears enforcing economic reprisals, legal repression, and violence for any reason.

Numerous court cases preceded *Brown v. Board of Education* (1954), and by 1952, the Supreme Court agreed to hear five cases related to school desegregation collectively. The grouping implied that school segregation affected the nation and not entirely in southern states. May 17, 1954, the Supreme Court ruled that the plaintiffs were "deprived of the equal protection of the laws guaranteed by the 14th Amendment." In May 1955, the Supreme Court issued a second opinion in the case known as *Brown v. Board of Education II*. Finally, the Supreme Court remanded future desegregation cases to lower federal courts and directed district courts and school boards to proceed "with all deliberate speed."

After Brown

The nation's reaction to *Brown* destroyed the careers of Black Career Educators. Northern communities hired white teachers and excluded Black Career Educators from employment options outside the Black community. Black Career Educators were fired, dismissed, and demoted, especially Black male teachers and principals, whom whites did not want working with white students. For example, in 1963, there were 227 Black high-school principals in North Carolina. In 1970, only eight Black principals remained in public schools. There was no reaction or concern by the white community to secure their jobs (Oakley et al., 2009).

The resistance to desegregate public schools destroyed career options for over 38,000 Black Career Educators in the southern states as well as southern border states. As if they were deked, they were suddenly unemployed. White school boards decided to close Black high schools, convert Black high schools to junior high schools, and change the name of schools named after Blacks (Oakley et al., 2009).

Southern school districts had the power to refuse the renewal of teaching contracts for

Black Career Educators, and some southern states established a different passing scale for Black and white teachers on the National Teachers Examination. While dismissing Black Career Educators varied according to school district size, large school districts fired as many as 3,000 Black educators, whereas in small school districts they fired as many as 25 Black Career Educators. Those who were not fired, were demoted (Oakley et al., 2009).

Desegregation presented a radical transformation to southern communities and required whites to exact their resistance to Black Career Educators regardless of the psychological, economic, and long-term implications. Desegregation allowed the very people who opposed desegregation to create new racially based policies and laws to control desegregation.

As the impact of the *Brown* decision destroyed Black Career Educators, structural racism continued to validate the belief that Black educators were poorly educated and trained (Fairclough, 2007). While *Brown* stimulated the nation's Civil Rights Movement, by no means did *Brown* change structural racism in public education. From day one, *Brown I and II* were deconstructed by elements of structural racism. In all regions of the United States, laws and policies were created to advance segregation, especially housing segregation that forced people of color into isolated enclaves and their children into more deeply segregated schools.

After 65 years, we know that efforts to desegregate public schools dismantled the careers of Black Career Educators and continues to destroy chances for students of color to receive equality in their public school education. In 2020, more than half of America's public school teachers are eligible to retire, and this option decreases the number of Black Career Educators and teachers of color in public education. Once this generation of educators is no longer in the schoolhouse, no one will replace them and advocate for students of color.

Supported by influences of structural racism, children of color in the twenty-first century attend resegregated schools, live in segregated communities laced with poverty, do not receive an education that links them to the future of work, and are gravely influenced by the current economic structure. A structure that allows whites to build an enormous wealth gap between people of color and isolate their children into wealthy school districts and communities.

3 THE COLOR OF CHAOS

Reality 101

I authored a dissertation in 1997, which concentrated on educational inequality, Black students, and their relationship with the nation's economy, as measured by unemployment, poverty, and high school attainment rates. In a 30-year historical materialist analysis, (1965-1995), historical materialism determines if a society's economic organization determines its social institutions and especially the relationship between the mode of production and the relationship between people in terms of economic production (Calhoun, 2012). Historical materialism looks at economic production, who owns the factories, and who works in the factories. This research study indicated that Black students increasingly completed more and more years of secondary education with the belief that educational attainment directly links to life-sustaining employment and economic well-being. However, data indicated that Black youth experienced increased levels of unemployment and consistently elevated levels of poverty during the research period.

Combined with nationwide and global decreases in wages, working-class Black youth completing high school faced polarization from wealth. Ironically, in 2020, the wealth gap between Black and white families and the economic divide between rich and poor individuals, is still enormous, and continues to expand.

America's economic system has a historical legacy of consciously creating racist policies and systems that economically oppress people of color. With the structural use of slavery, Jim Crow laws, housing and school segregation, income inequality and, more recently, mass incarceration, young people of color continue to experience social stratification that determines their wealth, income, education, and power in society.

Changes in economic production influences the restructuring of public school education in society to support the current economy. In wealthy communities, the academic curriculum in public schools aligns with the current economy, the future of work, and overall economic expectations of the community. However, for students of color, who attend resegregated public schools, schools lack resources to support multiple levels of cognitive engagement, and curriculums are not designed to advance their knowledge and skills related to the workforce, current economy, and the future of work.

In 1933, Carter G. Woodson argues that the so-called modern education met the needs of those who enslaved and oppressed weaker peoples (Woodson, 1933). Historically, the role of public education for Blacks and particularly that of segregated schools, was to provide only the necessary skills for Blacks to enter their intended place in society. Desegregated public schools challenged the belief of those who wanted to continue the economic oppression of Blacks.

The resegregation of public schools aligns with race-based policies that remove academic opportunities for students of color, and decrease their academic abilities and skill level needed to enter the workforce in global automation and technology-driven economies. Thus, the ultimate question— whether public school inequalities permanently destroy education as the great equalizer for students of color, especially Black and Hispanic students.

Teaching in Chaos

In the 1990s, I taught Black high school students from mostly working-class and low-income families. Even with a high school diploma, they were likely to be unemployed, underemployed, and have no access to financial resources to complete postsecondary education or job training. When cohesive links between educational attainment and the labor force are absent, students lose interest in obtaining an education. In communities where students of color see the impact of high rates of poverty, unemployment, underemployment, living conditions in isolated segregated housing, and attend segregated majority public schools, they cannot imagine a transition from the schoolhouse to life- sustaining employment and economic well-being. Instead, more profound social and psychological scars embed in a student's daily encounters and often, break down their coping skills.

Collectively, chaotic realities transform school cultures, school climates, and further fragment public school environments designed by structural racism. These are practices that both endure and adapt based solely on color.

Sixty-five years after *Brown* failed to desegregate public schools and destroyed options for Black Career Educators, the professional journeys of Black Career Educators are an entanglement of social and psychological inequalities that students of color painfully record in their memories and bring into their classrooms. I started teaching in 1985, and after 35 years, I will exit the chaos that consumes public education, the failure of *Brown* to desegregate public schools and provide equality in education, and the racism in higher education that attempts to define my intellectual abilities.

In Living Color

The following vignettes are a collection of over 35 years of vivid realities inside public schools where students of color remain covered in the persistence of racial inequality and educational experiences that provide no prospects for their future well-being. Racial disparities embedded by institutional racism never address the seriousness of their social-psychological encounters in resegregated neighborhoods and public schools.

He is tall and a very handsome young man. His nature is soft-spoken and calm. After several verbal suggestions to remove his cap, he refuses. Finally, I remove his cap, and he smiles. After school, he enters my classroom, and politely asks for his cap. Later in the school year, I learn that he is a major drug dealer in the neighborhood. He is a middle school student.

The mother is missing, and it is Christmas day. His grandmother calls and discovers that her daughter is missing, and the oldest grandson and his two siblings are living alone, in the dark, and the only food they receive is at school. The oldest grandson, in the 5th grade, has managed to take his siblings to school and take care of them on the weekend for over a month.

One day she is softly crying in class and unable to focus. I learn that she lives with her grandmother, and her uncle, who lives in the same household, has raped her. Her grandmother tells her to get over it. The next week she is absent and has been admitted to a local mental health hospital, where she is diagnosed as having a nervous breakdown at 15 years old.

I am in the courthouse for jury duty, and I recognize her face. She is the mother of a former student. I hear her conversation..."He won't be back...I wonder what he needs... that's my baby boy." Her baby boy's has been sentenced to 20 years in prison for murder in the 9th grade.

At night she roams the streets of the city because she hates going home to a lonely, small apartment. Her father stays with his girlfriend and comes by to leave her money to buy food.

After school, he runs home to claim his spot. Six people are staying in a one-bedroom apartment. If he does not go home early enough, he will sleep on the floor.

He will not take his science fair board home, so he explains that he cannot walk home with a science fair board. The boys in the neighborhood will beat him, so he comes to my classroom during his lunch period to finish his project.

He is so skinny that sideways you would not see him. He is absent for two months and finally walks into my classroom. He was shot ten times and lived.

It is summer, and school will open in a few weeks. He is short and walks toward my car while I am waiting at a red light. A former student, we exchange greetings and niceties. He asks, "How old are your sons?" I assume I will see him in September but in October, he shot and killed a Black couple driving on the freeway. He felt like killing someone. He receives life in prison.

He receives a full scholarship to play college football after graduating from high school. During the summer, he waits for a bus. Someone shoots him in the knee, shattering his patella, and he never attends college.

He is sleeping in his dorm room when someone knocks on the door. He opens his dorm room door. It is 2 a.m. The individual at the door shoots the wrong person. He dies.

I know the difference between firecrackers and gunshots. He ran into the school building, passed my classroom door, and another young man shot three times. He lives.

A young man enters the building and walks into the cafeteria. Using a book bag to collect the bullet casings, he shoots and kills one student.

I am rushing to pick up my sons at school. The police officer instructs me to drive my car through an alley. There are bullet casings on the street near my car. I inform the officer that I am not going through the alley, and finally, she relents but reminds me not to run over the bullet casings.

It is 8:30 in the morning. I need to enter the school building to avoid being late for work. I rush in and sign in. I walk to my classroom, take off my coat, and I remember to call the police. There is a dead body next to my car.

I am a high school tennis coach and retrieve my racquets from my car. I hear the gunshots and duck behind the school's marquee. It is another drive- by shooting.

She tells her mother she is gay, and her mother beats her into submission. She spends the night at a friend's house. Her mother refuses to give her money and coming to school depends on getting a ride from friends. Just like watching the seasons change, they go away and leave memories.

He is like a son. He is kind, intelligent, resilient, and indicates he will achieve and succeed in life. As he exits the building every day, he stops by my classroom to say goodbye. He receives a full scholarship from a prestigious university that will pay for his undergraduate and graduate education to become a physician. He dies in his sleep. It is the first student's funeral I attend and the last. The president *of the university, the high school principal, his teachers, his friends, and his family are present. With dark sunglasses to hide my swollen eyes, I clutch my husband's arm and tremble through the service. I leave before the service ends, always thinking, why? I have forgotten so many students, but I will remember this student forever. It still hurts.*

He has a football scholarship to a small southwestern college. I debate about sharing what I know. Do I have the right to tell him anything about the environment he will enter? He is academically strong but a Black man about to enter a white university where his white classmates are likely to fear Black men. Do I have the right to explain racism to this young Black man? He leaves the southwestern college, attends his state university, and completes his degree in engineering. When I see him, he tells me about the racist experiences and why he left the southwestern college.

The Psychology of Teaching

It seemed like an excellent idea, a fantastic way to bring closure to a psychology lesson. I pass out index cards and consistently remind students not to place their names on the index cards. Finally, I give the directions to list three things you do not want anyone to know about your life, and on the other side, list three things you want to share about your life. I collect over 150 cards, and the following are a representative sample of their most poignant thoughts:

I used to torture and kill animals, and I wanted to kill everyone at school

I was molested, and my father struggles with crack and other drugs

My mother is dead, and I am bipolar

I have so much anger built up inside

I am not sure who is my Dad, I used to cut my wrist, and I want to die

32

My family members struggle with drug addiction, my father has never given me any gifts, and sometimes I become depressed and emotional for no reason

I sometimes think that certain people's lives would be better if I were not alive

I must see a therapist due to my depression and aggression

I'm scared of abandonment...me being confused about my sexuality...I used to be depressed when I was younger

I love sex, I was raped, I have gay moments

I lost my mother, my father, and grandmother in the same year and I'm scared of touching

I was sexually molested

I watched my mom get abused when I was little for 3 years straight and I'm scared that I will end up like my mom

I used to be depressed and I was molested as a child

I struggled with depression last year and I used to self-harm

I was molested as a child by my uncle

I'm very depressed, I cry myself to sleep, and used to cut myself…I sometimes see things and I'm scared of the dark

I've been beaten and I get nervous in front of a lot of people…sometimes and I black out and don't notice

Low self-esteem, adopted, lonely, not happy, and always thinking negative

I cry a lot from stress and I like girls (the ones who look like boys)

I have mood swings a lot, I sometimes get emotional just because, and I hold a lot of things inside

I feel like I don't fit in with my family and that I'm different...I might have a mental illness

I was touched by my brother when I was little and this summer I overdosed and got really sick because I didn't want to attend school anymore

I'm depressed, I have low self-esteem, I was abused for most of my childhood life, and I think my father might have a mental illness

I have trouble sleeping every night and I feel pain in my chest very often

I cry a lot when I'm alone, I've thought about suicide before, and I'm not really happy with my life

I hear other people in my head, I see things, and I like to be alone in the dark all the time

I don't care if you get mad when I cut you up

I don't want people to know that I always feel ugly, that I cry almost every night, and that my Dad doesn't want me

As a teacher, I encounter raw edges exhibited by students confronting mental health issues that severely impact their academic progress and contribute to students dropping out of school. In a classroom, at any given time, at least one or two students are dealing with severe psychosocial stressors related to domestic violence, poverty, abuse, neglect, trauma, and other psychiatric disorders.

The daily challenges that students experience spill into hallways and illustrate their inability to regulate behaviors, emotions, social norms, and academic standards. The failure to recognize their harmful practices and actions contribute to outbursts, cursing, and defiance toward individuals of authority. In some cases, the students are oblivious to consequences related to their behaviors.

Consistently argumentative, students confront teachers, threaten teachers, and without one ounce of logic in their argument refuse to relent until they obtain the desired result.

As the school year progresses, teachers dread encountering students who exhibit negative behaviors in and outside classrooms.

Imagine three or five students who purposely derail every lesson or students in the hallway who act as though teachers are invisible and seldom alter their negative or inappropriate behaviors. There are students who, without hesitation, call a teacher a bitch, tell teachers to fuck off, and as one Black male student decided, while walking out the classroom, "Nigger be quiet."

Students defiantly bring marijuana into the schoolhouse, smoke it, and sell it without hesitation. Imagine entering a professional workspace at 8 a.m. and the smell of non-organic marijuana consumes your professional environment.

Daily encounters with individuals who experience social, economic, and educational disparities manifest for Black Career Educators as devastation and extreme stress. When students disregard established schoolhouse culture, disrespect figures of authority, and show no concern for consequences, then elements in their social environment reinforce behaviors that naturally transfer to the schoolhouse.

Neither administrators nor teachers are equipped to address systemic changes in society that students of color encounter when they travel through segregated communities and resegregated school hallways, knowing both consciously and unconsciously that the future of work does not exist. Their economic future has been replaced by intelligent machines, high-tech automation production, global commerce, and less need for their labor, even if they finish high school.

Ironically and so often, the administrative resolve for student issues points to more professional development for teachers on how to alter student behaviors, including introducing teachers to innovative approaches that can assist students with achieving their potential or novel approaches to understanding what creates and drives behaviors in students. Convincing teachers that they need more effective strategies to intervene before student behaviors are entrenched does not address or solve frustrations associated with poverty, imprisonment, unemployment, violence, and mental illness. This belief that classroom teachers can correct psychosocial stressors is ludicrous.

What I experienced as a Black Career Educator started in 1985. But in 2020, the realities of secondary and higher education are far more dramatic and devastating to watch in living color. These realities represent layers of inequalities woven by structural racism into public education for students of color. A more permanent form of racism, the cruelest, has evolved and lingers in the hallways while transforming school climates and cultures into an identical replica of segregated communities designed by economic despair and poverty. The freedom to express racism toward professors of color is rampant and develops as a norm on predominately white college campuses. As white college administrators dismiss and devalue concerns expressed by professors of color, the number of race-based incidents is increasing.

Criminalization and Students of Color

The nature of structural racism is such that it creates systemic chaos, especially in segregated communities and schools. This type of chaos changes school culture and the resulting chaos criminalizes students of color and students with disabilities.

Recently, the U.S. Department of Education required public schools in each state to report the number of social workers, nurses, and psychologists employed. The report provides essential data concerning both school-based mental health personnel and law enforcement in schools (American Civil Liberties Union, 2019). The data include disparities by race, disability status, and the fact that public schools are far more likely to be under-resourced and students over-criminalized.

It is highly essential to recognize that a student's social environment transfers to the schoolhouse, and if most students attending public schools are children of color and their community environments are deteriorating, imagine the impact on school climates. According to the American Civil Liberties Union (2019), data from both the U.S. Department of Education and the Centers for Disease Control and Prevention indicate that school children in the United States experience a record level of anxiety, depression, and trauma. Suicide rates among school-age children increased by 70 percent between 2002 and 2016, and 72 percent of children in the United States have experienced at least one major stressful event by witnessing acts of violence, abuse, and loss of loved ones before they finish high school.

Students who live in low-income and impoverished communities and attend schools in the same communities are far more likely to encounter elements of stress and trauma, and to act out in the schoolhouse. At the same time, schools that employ school-based mental health providers (nurses, social workers, psychologists, and school counselors) show improved attendance rates, lower suspension rates, lower disciplinary incident rates, and expulsions. Schools with adequate ratios of students to school-based mental health providers enhance academic achievement, career opportunities, and graduation rates (Laban et al., 2012).

School-based mental health providers improve health outcomes and school safety (Cleveland and Sink, 2017). Even though school-based mental health professionals, who provide support services to students, cannot single-handedly improve a student's community environment, their professional skills support and transfer to students by introducing alternative methods and coping mechanisms for generating positive outcomes—a process that can stabilize and save lives.

Nearly 35 million students have experienced at least one childhood trauma, and 72 percent of students experience at least one traumatic event before the age of 18. Mental health issues that emerge during adolescence, a timeframe for the most effective treatments, are not identified or treated for any number of reasons. In addition, 1 in 10 youth may require additional support from schools (Stagman & Cooper, 2010).

Meanwhile, the financial support for police in schools has increased, yet nationwide there is an alarming shortage of funding for school-based mental health providers. Ironically, the presence of police officers in public schools does not improve school safety and in numerous cases, causes more harm. Detaining, handcuffing, and arresting students in the schoolhouse increases student alienation and creates a poor school climate. Historically, marginalized students of color attend public schools with fewer academic resources. Adding law enforcement to public schools compounds the educational inequities and further increases the criminalization of students of color given that schools with police report nearly four times as many arrests as schools without police officers (Civil Rights Data Collection, 2019).

Disproportionately, public schools arrest students of color and students with disabilities. Nationwide, the overall arrest rate for students stands at 28 per 10,000 Black students arrested, 11 per 10,000 Hispanic students arrested, and 9 per 10,000 white students arrested (Department of Education, 2015- 2016, CRDC). For students with disabilities, the arrest rate stands at 29 per 10,000 students, which is three times higher than their non-disabled peers (Department of Education, 2015-2016, CRDC).

For schools without police officers, the arrest rate of students with disabilities stands at 17 per 10,000 students arrested. In contrast, for schools with police officers, the arrest rate of 51 per 10,000 for students with disabilities (Department of Education, 2015-2016, CRDC).

According to the American Civil Liberties Union (2019):

- 2 million students are in schools with police officers but no counselors;
- Three million students are in schools with police officers but no nurses;
- Six million students are in schools with police officers but no school psychologists;
- Ten million students are in schools with police officers but no social workers;

- Fourteen million students are in schools with police officers but no counselor, nurse, psychologists, or social worker.

The minimum staffing recommendations and requirements suggest one counselor and one social worker for every 250 students, one nurse for every 750 students, and one psychologist for every 700 students. The sad reality is that 90 percent of public schools fail to meet the minimum staffing recommendations for school-based mental health providers. However, the number of law enforcement officers in public schools is 2-3 times greater than social workers, and at least five states reported more police officers in public schools than nurses (ACLU, 2019).

New Tools

Sixty-five years since *Brown I and II,* extraordinarily little has changed for children of color in public schools. Public schools are nothing more than a direct link to social and economic inequalities found in our society; they prepare students of color for less-skilled, routine jobs, obedience, and acceptance of authority and external control (Irvine, 1991).

The education of America's children was cultivated on the premise of integration into our economic society. Naturally, changes in the transformation of an economy coincide with the focus placed on education, as well as notable shifts in skill requirements. Economic changes have led to changes in the educational system, and some scholars believe schools are merely tools manipulated by individuals with wealth and power (Shorten, 2014.).

Curriculum is a perfect tool to control inequality in public schools, especially along the lines of class. School curricula can control which life-sustaining skills are taught, and which skills will align with the future of work. According to Anyon (1980), students from different economic classes receive different knowledge in public schools. Based on the expected outcomes, tracking students can determine who goes to college, career choice, general education, and each track leads to drastically different career possibilities. Du Bois' metamorphosis on education and the Black race concluded that Black students were victims who have been hurt and crushed by oppressive racial laws, policies, and practices (Du Bois, 1973). This truth is never more evident than in the Black journey to receive equality in public education.

Initially, education was denied to Blacks, then segregated, and in the twenty-first century the journey to equality in public education is resegregated, laced with mental illness, and criminalization. Despite new tools in structural racism that evolve over time with the same intent, equal opportunity to education for people of color will never exist without the influence of structural racism.

Educational policies support the economic system in which children of color enter. And while some scholars believe in human capital and thus the belief that one's family background or social class does not place limits on individuals if they invest in themselves, one can only ask where are children of color and their families supposed to find funding to transform their lives? Resegregation in schools and communities compounded by poverty, psychosocial stressors, unemployment, underemployment, low minimum wages, s, increased housing costs, higher cost to achieve a college degree or career training, and school inequalities do not provide financial links to human investment and the future of work. Certainly, the prevalent poverty levels for children of color impose social, cognitive, health-related, and stress-related challenges on students every day, and all these factors affect students' ability to learn. But understand, poverty creates a sense of hopeless, passive behaviors, and isolation, while cultivating bursts of violence. All elements that consistently exist in a wealthy society in order to advance and secure white power.

As a sociologist, I look at what school environments provide for children of color especially at the high school level where I spent over 20 years as a Black Career Educator. I have observed the behaviors of students and the truths in the daily routines of students and school culture, which serves as a socialization process. Recently, the socialization process for students of color portrays a dramatic dynamic between segregated environments in which students live and the systematic elimination of opportunities to college, careers, and the future of work. The results are hostile behaviors and psychological damage that no one in the schoolhouse can address without acknowledging the influence of structural racism. While changes in school culture are recognized at a school administrative level, the necessary talents to address changes are elusive. Structural changes in the United States economy, especially increases in the wealth gap between whites and people of color, no longer simply limit or reduce opportunities for people of color to enter the workforce. Instead, those opportunities have been eliminated. Thus, high school climates reflect social conditions indicating that high school diplomas no longer support economic well-being and a quality lifestyle for students of color but are designed with mental illness and criminalization as a permanent outcome.

4 REALITIES IN THE SCHOOLHOUSE

When Teachers are Mentally Ill

As a teacher, I cannot select which students I prefer to engage with and teach. I can only assume that parents do not keep their perfect children at home and thus, send the less than ideal children to school. Either way, students can consciously and unconsciously create stressful environments and demonstrate an assortment of misbehaviors that equally contribute to teacher burnout and mental breakdowns. Regardless of the teaching environment, both rural, suburban, and urban school districts are contenders for causing teacher burnouts and mental stress.

Increasingly, the best and idealistic school environments and communities experience gun violence. The constant thought that violence can enter a schoolhouse and remove the joy of teaching is a grim reality for American teachers. Some, more than others, are heartbreaking to the very core of your soul. I will never forget the shooting at Sandy Hook Elementary School on December 14, 2012, in Newtown, Connecticut. That day 20 elementary school children, between the ages of six and seven, and six staff members were killed.

Teacher Mental Health in the United States

In 1955, developmental psychologists McKee and Jersild encouraged teacher-training programs to address teacher conflicts and anxieties. Jersild was concerned about the well-being of teachers and how school environments encourage feelings of loneliness, alienation, and guilt. Roger Hock (1988) observed in a questionnaire study that variables such as job stress, dissatisfaction, psychological effects of burnout, and related physical symptoms contributed to professional burnout. School boards, administrators, and teachers knew about these variables and their impact on American school systems, but solutions were not a concern.

The professional nuisances of teaching are not strange; however, they are unique to the profession as Hock identified five (5) causes of teacher burnout:

1. Being trapped in the profession
2. Difficulties with classroom discipline
3. Isolation from colleagues
4. Lack of support related to professional issues
5. Lack of support related to personal problems

As to what can cause mental illness, especially among teachers, it varies. Initially, teachers may dismiss early signs of mental illness and attribute health issues to just the nature of the profession or assume that they are not severe enough to be labeled as mental illness. However, according to the American Federation of Teachers (2015), in an 80-question survey completed by more than 30,000 educators, 78 percent of teachers experienced physical and emotional exhaustion at the end of the day. Teachers indicated that their major workforce stressors included not only students but factors such as the adoption of new initiatives without training, mandatory professional development, mandated curriculum initiatives, and standardized testing. All of these factors that can contribute to stress-related illnesses and depression.

The number of teachers dealing with mental health issues increases each year, and teachers attribute mental health problems to excessive demands associated with the profession. Furthermore, few educators discuss or disclose their health problems with administrators or have opportunities to seek professional counseling within their school districts. Teachers who are managing their mental health are often linked to shame, fear, feeling ostracized, incompetence, and the stigma of mental illness, which can be a professional liability.

Subsequently, school districts that investigate mental health issues related to teachers discover that teachers are dealing with drug and alcohol abuse, aggressive behaviors toward colleagues and students, depression, anxiety, bipolar disorders, and post-traumatic stress disorder. Ironically, after identifying teacher mental health issues, professional support for teachers is not a priority in most school districts, and teachers may or may not know how to seek professional help or contact a mental health professional, provided that they have a health care plan that covers mental illness. Career educators are likely to experience stress and emotional exhaustion during their teaching career and each school year, more teachers exhibit signs of mental illness, and they are not fully aware of their mental illness.

The National Institute of Mental Health states that one in five children experience a severe mental disorder, and half of all people with mental disorders will have an onset of their illness by age 14 (Mental Illness, 2019). Astonishingly, teachers are highly likely to interact with a multitude of school-age children who deal with mental illness, trauma, and emotional needs. All these health issues require shrewd professional training to recognize.

Nationwide most educators receive mandated professional development training related to reporting student sexual abuse, extensive professional development in recognizing emotional and mental health issues in students, and training related to basic first aid. Although, knowing how to recognize and address teacher mental health issues is not a priority in most public school districts, despite the fact that teachers are essential individuals in a student's life.

The mental illness crisis related to educators is not a crisis only in the United States. Educators in both European and Asian countries experience significant levels of job stress and the psychological effects of burnout, especially in some of the most prestigious school systems.

International Teachers and Mental Health

In 1978, British teachers with psychotic or psychoneurotic illness had prolonged exposure to students and in some cases, for years (MacAnespie, 1978). The range of diseases included paranoia, failure to relate to colleagues, aggressiveness, and hallucinations. British Community Medical Specialists from 1967 to 1973 interviewed 36 teachers, of which 17 experienced relapses of a chronic condition, 19 suffered from a mental illness, or had a history of mental breakdowns. Interestingly, 21 of the teachers appeared to have some insight into their mental health (MacAnespie, 1978; Kyriacou, 1987).

In one British case study, a teacher was absent for five weeks (without explanation) then returned and stated to the director of education that he traveled abroad seeking treatment for his venereal disease. Later, a medical examination indicated he did not have a venereal disease. Numerous interviews with the individual supported a paranoid personality, delusions of persecution, and eccentric behaviors. Sadly, he refused a psychiatric examination before dismissal after protesting outside his former school and the department of education. The study concluded that some teachers are unsuited for a teaching profession, and others have drifted into teaching to discover they are at risk for mental illness (MacAnespie, 1978).

Job stress continues to overwhelm teachers in the United Kingdom, and according to Sellgren (2016), teachers are experiencing either physical or mental conditions that are work-related. Research in 2016 by the Education Support Partnership supported the same claim. Their research indicated that 75 percent of the teaching staff in both schools and colleges experienced work-related depression, anxiety, and panic attacks.

The British education system, often replicated worldwide, holds tremendous prestige. However, decades of research indicate that teacher mental health concerns implicitly impact the delivery of their award-winning curriculum and confirms the global crisis related to mental health issues and the teaching profession. Likewise, in Japan, Singapore, and Hong Kong, education systems maintain high academic standards. However, despite the emphasis on curriculum standards, teachers in all three countries experience elevated levels of mental illness.

In Japan, teachers serve beyond their classroom content area as directors of after-school programs and visit student homes to gather an understanding of family dynamics. Japanese teachers are likely to work over 63 hours a week and are not compensated for overtime.

In 2011, the Tokyo Times reported that 5,000 Japanese teachers had a mental illness related to depression and other psychiatric disorders. According to Shorton (2014), the Japan Education Ministry conducted a study in 2013. The study indicated that 62 percent of teachers in all levels of public schools took leave for depression or other mental illnesses, and the number of mentally ill teachers in Japan doubled in 10 years. While psychological health support for Japanese students has increased, there is no indication that teachers receive support beyond their own interventions, and a few schools and local authorities provide rehabilitation support programs for teachers.

Subramaniam et al., 2012, indicates that according to The Singapore Mental Health Study, 12 percent of the population—or 1 in 8 people—have a mental disorder. The most common disorders are depression, alcohol abuse, and obsessive-compulsive disorders. Released in 2014, The Hong Kong Mental Morbidity Survey (a primary territory-wide assessment) states that 1 in 6 residents has a common mental disorder (anxiety or depression). With a population of over 7 million and growing, according to Heifetz (2016), the Hong Kong College of Psychiatrists indicates that there are only 345 psychiatrists, and each patient competes with 20,000 others for an appointment.

In 2016 the Teaching and Learning International Survey (TALIS) stated that Singapore has a young teaching population with fewer years of experience. Overall, the survey indicated that teachers work in isolation, seldom team-teach with colleagues, and seldom observe their colleagues teaching. One can conclude that given the youthful age of Singapore teachers (average age 36 years) and naturally, a lack of teaching experience combined with an average work week of 56 hours, teachers in Singapore are highly likely to experience high rates of mental disorders. This situation is compounded by the emotional health of students, which is a significant concern for many schools in recent years.

The Education Bureau and the Department of Health in Singapore (2016), increased student awareness and understanding of mental health by launching the Joyful@HK Campaign. The campaign aims to promote mental well-being and disseminate information about mental health using radio programs, social media, school-based activities, and professional development training for teachers.

Globally, the most significant volume of scholarly research focuses on the mental health of children. Research about educators and mental health is not a priority area of research even though globally, teachers have an array of severe mental health issues.

The Color of Mental Illness

In the United States, there is a significant decline in the number of individuals choosing to enter the teaching profession, and school systems are anticipating significant shortages in teachers. At the same time, the duties assigned to teachers expand each year to include more and more responsibilities while the mental and emotional health of teachers suffers from neglect. In fact, several school districts are offering mental health first aid courses for teachers. These courses are designed to train teachers to recognize early signs of mental distress in students. Once again, teacher mental health is not a priority.

Take a moment to reflect historically and consider the long history associated with the education of Blacks in America. The fear of lynching for teaching Blacks to read and write, the refusal to educate Blacks before and after the Civil War, and at the dawn of *Brown*, economic policies designed as defiant reactions to enforcing *Brown* included racism, and discrimination in employment, especially during economic recessions. For Black Career Educators, prejudice and the elimination of their jobs, enforced with economic policies, destroyed their opportunities to obtain economic stability. So, imagine the psychological stress of losing a job, being forced into unemployment, loss of family income, the lost opportunities to build generational wealth, and white teachers with fewer qualifications taking their jobs. Imagine the wretched heartache internalized by Black Career Educators.

For the first time in America's history, students of color are the majority population entering public schools, and most teachers in American (80 percent) are white and female. The dynamics of this interaction are not necessarily favorable for students of color. This is a momentous challenge for white teachers trying to create culturally relevant experiences, raising their expectations for students of color, and not avoiding conversations about race to marginalize students of color further.

It is a known fact that more students of color are referred for special education evaluations, stereotyped as having behavioral problems, labeled as not being interested in school, and as the cause of low school performance on a standardized test. With the majority of Black Career Educators retiring, the only plausible replacements are white female teachers who will enter segregated and resegregated public schools with the majority ethnic population. Naturally, one wonders if this factor advances mental health issues for white female teachers who teach majority ethnic populations and complicates the emotional dynamics of public education for students of color — the very students who experience the highest levels of mental health issues.

Mental Health and Black Children

For Blacks in the United States, the history of mental illness undoubtedly intertwines with structural racism and racist attitudes. As early as 1848, physician John Galt believed that Blacks were immune to mental illness. Enslaved people did not own property, vote, and engage in commerce, and thus, only white males were more likely to suffer mental illness, given their exposure to the stress of profit-making (Umeh, 2019). Furthermore, physicians believed Black slaves suffered from negritude, the desire to become white, while others thought it was unusual for Africans to experience mental illness after becoming slaves. Still other white physicians believed the treatment of depression, lethargy, or dullness required severe whipping (Umeh, 2019).

Naturally, after the Civil War, segregation prevented the treatment of whites and Blacks for mental illness in the same facilities. Consequently, the worst treatment descended upon Black children who were often misdiagnosed, mistreated, and forced into manual labor on farms located near mental institutions. White physicians believed that Black children's ability to sustain manual work supported their belief that Black children were not mentally ill since manual labor required skills (Umeh, 2019). Hence, white physicians seldom considered social conditions, economic depression, poverty, racial discrimination, rape, and the possibility of being lynched as contributors to the mental state of Blacks, especially after the Civil War (Umeh, 2019).

Regardless of where Blacks lived after the Civil War and well into the twentieth century, American institutions disregarded Black mental health or practiced extreme medical procedures on Blacks. As an illustration, in California, North Carolina, and Alabama, Black women were disproportionately sterilized when they were misdiagnosed, falsely accused of crimes, and declared by courts to be mentally defective.

Additionally, from the 1930s to 1960s Blacks were victims of psychosurgery by white doctors, a surgical process used to remove parts of the brain (lobotomy) as a treatment for mental illness. Several white psychiatrists and neurosurgeons believed that urban violence and riots in the 1960s were not a reaction to systemic racism, poverty, and police brutality but a treatable brain disorder that generated Black violence. Thus, lobotomies performed on Black children, as young as five years old, provided a solution for demonstrated aggressive or hyperactive behaviors (Jackson, 2002).

Interestingly, an analysis of the historical, cultural, and social psychological aspects of mental health indicates how institutional racism intentionally allowed physicians to inhumanely practice medicine as it relates to Blacks and especially Black children. Furthermore, in the twenty-first century, our racialized society continues to create social and economic conditions that purposely destroyed the mental health of Black children. Most harrowing, the systemic destruction of their mental health initiates in public schools.

Social and Economic Impacts on Well-Being

The perpetuation of racism and inequality is endless. For Black children, social, economic, and mental health inequalities are combining in public schools and segregated communities to dismantle their well-being. A child's social and parental environments are essential and can serve as a crucial predictor of life experiences. Environments build elements associated with success, inspiration, and mobility (McAdoo, 2000). Nevertheless, when these elements are missing, Black children are forced to live in environments that exude multiple levels of poverty, segregation, and isolation. The impact is often a permanent mental stressor. Besides, social-economic status (SES) is a critical factor in mental health, and naturally determines access to psychological resources. According to Meyers (2009), SES intersects with social and environmental factors and collectively forms an extraordinarily complex interaction of factors, including poverty and race.

Likewise, childhood adversities link to mental disorders and impact children of color at a higher rate. According to Kessler et al., 2007, childhood adversities include trauma, stress, pollution, poor housing, lack of education, low SES, exposure to violence, discrimination, prejudice, and stereotyping that eventually influences a child's health and mental health outcomes (Keenan et al., 2012).

It is common for a child's family structure to contribute to mental illness and childhood disparities. According to Green et al., 2010, who references The National

Comorbidity Replication Survey, childhood adversities can be linked back to parental mental illness, family violence, physical abuse, sexual abuse, neglect, and substance abuse. Additionally, most Black children live in single-parent female households (67 percent) and are less likely to receive support from institutions that facilitate parenting support and thus, the reduction of childhood adversity (Kids Count Data Center, 2014). The issue is not about Black children raised by single mothers but the fact that single female households are likely to have low income levels and therefore, fewer resources. On the other hand, single-parent male households have more expendable income than female single-parent households, and thus, this factor can decrease childhood adversities and mental health problems (Alderman & Battle, 2000).

In addition to family structure, there is consistent evidence about the influence of a child's neighborhood that can contribute to mental health outcomes. Given that Black children are highly likely to live in high-poverty, segregated neighborhoods with elevated levels of concentrated disadvantages, their chances of experiencing various forms of mental illness increase (Casciano and Massey, 2012). Subsequently, residential segregation is exceptionally central to disparities—disparities that can influence health outcomes for children of color given that segregated communities have higher levels of inequalities in education and a variety of risk factors such as violence, crime, and ambient noises (Sampson et al., 2002).

Without question, environments with social disorganization, economic deprivation, crowding, discrimination, and marginalization are psychological stressors for both children and adults. This type of environment increases the probability of children and adolescents developing depression and a sense of detachment. Authors Singh and Ghandour (2012), indicate that children and adolescents ages 6-17, who live in the worst neighborhoods, had two times higher odds of serious behavioral problems. Children living in poverty had four times higher odds of serious behavioral problems when compared to children who did not experience these conditions. Thus, children of color are more likely to exhibit a wide range of adverse mental health outcomes because of family structure and environmental conditions.

Consequently, Black children and their families face the backlashes of retrenchment. Regardless of presumed progress from the passage of legislation, court rulings, and formal mechanisms that attempt to install racial equality, retrenchment erodes progress. For example, *Brown v. Board of Education of Topeka, Brown II,* and the Fair Housing Act aimed to promote racial equality. However, the nature of retrenchment creates a gradual erosion of progress. Retrenchments are especially evident when budget cuts in public education exert negative impacts on low-income school districts more so than middle-class school districts. Equally as devastating is the wealth gap between families of color and white families. In recent decades, trends in income inequality link to income-based achievement gaps that are greater than racially based achievement gaps. According to Reardon (2011), the achievement gap between children from high-income and low-income families is roughly 30 to 40 percent larger among children born in 2001. Thus, as the wealth gap increases, so will the achievement gap.

In the twenty-first century, Black children are consistent victims of institutional racism, criminalization, school discipline, poverty, low academic outcomes, unemployment, and they are far more likely to experience mental illness. In public schools, students of color (especially Blacks and Hispanics) are handcuffed and arrested, receive harsher discipline, and attend resegregated schools in isolated segregated communities. In resegregated schools, curricula intentionally develop low skill outcomes that place students of color in low paying jobs if not unemployment and underemployment—a combination that manifests in the schoolhouse and leads to mental stressors.

Childhood Suicide

The most catastrophic outcome of structural racism that impacts children of color is understanding that in 2017, more than a third of elementary school- aged suicides involved Black children (Centers for Disease Control and Prevention, 2017). Traditionally suicide rates were presumed to be higher among whites than Blacks across all age groups. However, new evidence shows that racial disparities in suicide rates for Black children ages 5-12 were two times higher than those of similarly aged children (Bridge et al., 2018).

Crossover to suicide deaths among Black teenagers and research indicates that for Black females aged 13-19, suicide rates rose 182 percent between 2001 and 2017. The rate among Black teenage males rose 60 percent during the same period. A significant factor that contributes to suicide rates among Black youth is discrimination. Compounded with anxiety, which can be precipitated by encounters with discrimination, internalized racism, and depression, Black youth are increasingly thinking about death (Walker, 2018).

Structural racism destroys the link to well-being for Black youth as they try to live in segregated communities, attend resegregated public schools, encounter white educators who practice deficit thinking, and they are not provided a path or link to prosperity in public schools.

Sunup to sundown...picking that cotton

Sunup to sundown...whipped by the massa

Sunup to sundown...chains and shackles

No more auction block for me...

No more auction block for me...

No more auction block for me... (Negro Spiritual)

Educational Achievement and Mental Illness

Most children growing up in poverty, living in racially segregated neighborhoods, and neighborhoods with an array of contextual factors are children of color. Collectively, this combination of social-economic factors increases their chance of developing mental illness. Thus, without success in educational achievement, students are less likely to experience social mobility and well-being.

In 1985 Comer and Hill wrote about the impingement of social, political, and economic policies on the mental health of Black children. The authors indicated that America's economic policies consistently, past and present, prevent Black families from obtaining an education and other resources necessary to establish adequate family functioning. In addition to the influence of economic and education policies, Black families are inordinately traumatized by housing and health care social policies that undeniably influence Black children who disproportionately present with learning disabilities and antisocial behavioral problems. With evidence that cognitive and social developmental problems among Black children are preventable, the necessary immensity of social programs is not available and suggest a lack of societal concern to solve the problem.

A child's mental health is a product of multiple interactions, and including interactions between their family members, environment, social networks, community, and other institutions in society. For Blacks, both the historical and current dynamics of oppression (social, political, and economic), and racism disproportionately remove resources that are essential to establish conditions for adequate family interaction and child development. Allocated with inequitable social and economic policies, institutional laws, and racist practices at state and local levels of government, Black families continue to endure the effects of racism and discrimination in the workforce that results in multigenerational poverty, and other social and mental health problems.

These types of conditions increase the probability of children living in stressful and inadequate income households without a sense of well-being, positive mental health, and psychological support, if needed.

While Medicaid plays a significant role in reducing health disparities for people of color, structural disparities such as lower education levels and higher rates of unemployment and underemployment reduce access to private healthcare insurance. The Medicaid and Children's Health Insurance Program (CHIP) provides healthcare for 28 percent of Black adults, 57 percent of Black children, 25 percent of Hispanic adults, and 58 percent of Hispanic children (CHIP, 2019). Subsequently, the historical, social, and psychological aspects of a racialized society are continuous and appear to be endless.

Generations of Blacks know the consequences of education and economic denials, which are often controlled by economic conditions and inadequate educational policies designed to hinder economic mobility and overall educational achievement. This extremely complex interaction harms Black families and their ability to provide more positive social climates and learning environments that do not jeopardize their children's mental health. This aspect is especially difficult for families living in segregated housing environments that do not offer social mobility or greater access to social resources.

The attempt of *Brown* to desegregate public schools increased the use of race-based education policies by state and local governments as well as white school districts that placed limitations on Black educational opportunities, achievement, and funding for segregated Black schools. Further, seldom discussed are the short- and long-term psychological effects on Black students attending desegregated schools where toxic psychological interactions and hostile school environments included physical and verbal attacks by teachers, administrators, students, and parents. For so many Blacks students, attending recently desegregated schools after the *Brown* decision meant encounters with teachers who assumed they were not intelligent and would be discipline problems, or did not want them in their classroom. According to Lyles 2013, in segregated schools, Black students were more likely to have caring Black teachers who perceived them as intellectually capable and motivated to succeed even though race-based policies tried to dismantle Black segregated schools and Black Career Educators.

Race-based policies are infused with psychologically damaging interactions that affected Black students' personal and professional life experiences. In 1945 author Richard Wright wrote *Black Boy*. Wright's childhood experiences in the South build an array of mental challenges centered around desertion, racism, and humiliation. All of these elements contribute to being cognizant of aspirations for a young Black man in the South. In 1965, Claude Brown wrote *Manchild in the Promised Land*, which portrays a young Black man growing up in Harlem in the 1940s and 1950s. Brown emphasized inner-city violence, despair, poverty, and the ghettoization of Blacks. His book portrays the stigmatization and degradation experienced by young Black men. The author illustrates how the influences and outcomes of gang violence, crime, lack of education, and mental distress challenged Black men with the lack of stability in their segregated urban community. When Maya Angelou wrote *I Know Why the Caged Bird Sings* in 1969, the brilliant author instantiates a young Black girl's life in America's landscape—a life filled with insecurity, the pain of feeling ugly, rejection and abandonment, and sexual molestation and rape. A life surrounded by racism can manifest in her daily life with indignities. Overall, the three novels articulate the quintessential stories of growing up Black in America under structural racism and inequitable policies, and practices that intentionally place Blacks at a disadvantage.

Whether depicting Black childhood traumas in the twentieth or twenty-first centuries, the consistent pattern of neglecting the need for mental health intervention in Black communities persists. In the twenty-first century, institutional racism (policies and practices) endure in school disciplinary policies that punish children of color as young as 3 years old and thus, create a path to the criminal justice system. Black children are far more likely to face the consequences and discipline associated with the misinterpretation of their behaviors, labeled aggressive, and thus their parents are assumed to be neglectful and remiss in their duty to acculturate their children to expected social norms. Their behaviors that are not analyzed from a psychological interpretation but from a negative cultural understanding or unconscious perception that children of color are criminals in the making.

As early as pre-K, healthy 3 year old behaviors for Black children are pathologized (labeled as abnormal), and thus 3 year old Black children are suspended or expelled from preschools. According to the Department of Education in 2013-2014, Black preschool students composed 19 percent of the preschool population yet received 48 percent of the suspensions or expulsions. Discipline policies that are racially inequitable, especially the zero-tolerance school discipline policies, push boys of color to the prison pipeline and girls of color to face discriminatory discipline actions in public schools.

According to the Department of Education (2014), Black students and students with disabilities are twice as likely to be suspended. Suspensions increase the likelihood of not graduating from high school, and Black males without a high school diploma interact with the criminal justice system at least once in their lives. This systemic pattern within society and public schools increases the encounters with mental toxicity for Black children and their families who regularly interact with the retrenchment of public policies. The maintaining of segregated neighborhoods, and the enforcement of inequalities in segregated public schools with majority ethnic populations are their reality.

There are critical times in which developing minds are vulnerable to the affects of experiencing poverty and adversity. Additionally, a broad range of factors, circumstances, and experiences impact childhood and adolescence. When societal toxins surround children of color, they experience poor nutrition, maltreatment, abuse, and a decreased ability to focus and cope with life. Interventions that address early childhood education, prenatal and infant nutrition, and helping low-income parents with stress and challenges related to raising young children to reduce the prevalence of behavioral health problems in both childhood and adolescence, as well as in adulthood, are not a priority supported by government agencies in resegregated communities. Children of color have a desperate need for interventions that can help prevent mental health problems in their communities and schools. Mental health disparities need interventions that improve conditions for children of color throughout their childhood and adolescence, and across environments regardless of where they live. These interventions must target the causes of mental health disparities in the social, economic, school, family, neighborhood, and health care contexts. We know that different settings shape the developing mind during an individual's childhood and attacking inequities eliminates long-term mental health issues in an individual's life and overall health conditions in society (Alegria et al., 2015).

Mental Health and Hispanic Children

By 2060, 119 million Hispanics will live in the United States Office of Minority Health, 2016). Currently, Hispanics represent 18 percent of the United States population, and making them the largest ethnic group, and the youngest population. Approximately one-third of the Hispanic population is under the age of 18, and half of Hispanics born in the United States are younger than 18 years of age (Patten, 2016). Sadly, this young population, especially Hispanic youth, are more likely to deal with mental health issues than their peers. Twenty-two percent of Hispanic youth have depressive symptoms, and according to the U.S. Office of Minority Health (2016), Hispanic adolescents have the highest rates of suicidal ideation and suicide attempts. Most suicide attempts occur before age 18, and Hispanic females are twice as likely to attempt suicide than males.

As a growing student population in public schools, Hispanic children and youth face stressors from issues related to immigration, poverty, cultural identity, bullying, and discrimination. Unfortunately, Hispanic children are not likely to receive support for mental health, and their parents are less likely to recognize or seek help for their children's mental health issues (Mental Health & Latino Kids, 2017). For Hispanic students, barriers to mental health services include cultural differences in perception of mental health and mistrust toward schools and medical professionals by their parents (Mental Health & Latino Kids, 2017).

Several research studies report significant findings related to depressive symptoms in Hispanic high school students and discrimination directed toward Hispanic students from other students and teachers in public schools (Lopez et al., 2016). According to Stacciarini et al., 2015, Hispanic adolescents reported feeling like outsiders when attending public schools and experienced overt racism and discrimination both in schools and their community. When adolescents lacked opportunities to participate in extracurricular activities, one of their stressors included not having after-school transportation. Several adolescents stated that the safest place in their community was the church.

Most students in public schools are children of color, especially Blacks and Hispanics. Racial and ethnic disparities in public school education increase annually and the growth and impact on Black and Hispanic children increases psychiatric inpatient and emergency department utilization rates, especially among Black children. Marrast et al., 2016, concluded that psychiatric and behavior problems for children of color often results in school punishment and incarceration, but seldom mental health care. While Hispanic children experienced lower hospitalization rates, regardless of their mental health impairment, demographics, and medical insurance status, racial and ethnic disparities occurred in outpatient care as well.

Racism and Student Mental Health

There is a general reluctance to identify structural racism as a catalyst in mental health related to children of color even though a historical legacy of racism in public education exists. While structural racism firmly aligns with educational practices in public schools, the impact on children of color manifests in educational practices, distribution of resources, discrimination, and psychological damage. Codified in public education with the use of laws, practices, and policies, the nature of structural racism unequivocally attributes to mental illness.

According to McAdoo (2000), racism as a force shapes both child development and psychological functioning. At the same time, the complexity of structural racism relegates children of color and their families to racial prejudice, oppression, and segregated communities (Garcia-Coll et al., 1996). Without question, the experiences of racism impact a child's cognitive and social development, and with health care disparities, children of color illustrate that mental health issues are increasing.

Mental breakdowns for children of color start incredibly early in their schooling journey. Given that most teachers in public schools are white females, and the majority of Black Career Educators are retiring, children of color are likely to have more frequent encounters with discrimination from white teachers. The discrimination that appears in the form of receiving lower grades or being disciplined more harshly as well as peer discrimination related to school activities (Wong et al., 2003). These experiences increase depressive symptoms, elevate anger, and often lead to children having low self-esteem as early as middle school.

As children of color reach adolescence, males are more likely to experience stereotyping and racial prejudice. In the schoolhouse, males of color receive less academic support and a disproportionate number of severe responses to violation of school rules. Structural racism inside a schoolhouse includes stereotyping, prejudice, and discrimination that destroys the ability to obtain educational equality — a structure that increases mental health challenges, and the ability to achieve life-sustaining employment and well-being.

Resegregation of public schools and communities of color creates environments that limit social capital for children of color and their ability to acquire the necessary skills and training needed to compete in a global society and the future of work. Individuals disenfranchised through discrimination lose access to skills and credentials for economic stability, cannot transfer family wealth, have limited or no social networks for support, and live in communities that do not offer economic opportunities. Nevertheless, children of color who are experiencing resegregated and economically disadvantaged schools, communities with epidemic poverty levels, and racially cultivated disparities are expected to pass standardized tests while slowly declining into the depths of mental darkness. The structural levels of racism slowly and permanently destroy mental health with psychological depression, suicide, anxiety, low self- esteem, risky behaviors, and criminalization. With limited access to mental health services in schools in resegregated communities, children of color and their parents are increasingly isolated while combating mental health issues.

5 AS I WALK AWAY

Cursing 101

While each generation of students has slang terms, the use of the word "fuck" in schools has become pervasive. Among high school students, it is used just as commonly as the words "cell" and "phone." In the 1960s, a common slang term, "Hippie," which according to the Merriam Webster Dictionary, means "derived from the term hipster; refers to an individual who rebels against established institutions and opposes the Vietnam War." A favorite slang word for a student of the 1970s was "copacetic," which means everything is excellent or exquisite. In the 1980s, students may have used the term "bodacious," meaning bold or impressive. Either way, being "cool" meant adopting the latest expression of thought but never turning curse words into a norm for dialogue in the schoolhouse.

It may seem unusual to discuss the usage of the work "fuck" from a scholarly perspective, and yet "fuck" is a common slang term implying to have sexual intercourse with someone or ruin and damage something. Although generally used as a verb to express one's annoyance and contempt, the word "fuck" can also be used as a noun; "the fuck." Increasingly used as a natural and familiar part of language expression, the term has a very flexible establishment in English grammar. For example, one can use the term as a noun, interjection, grammatical ejaculation (a quick utterance to indicate strong feelings), and both a transitive and intransitive verb. Hence, the use of the term dates to the early 1500s, but regardless of the history, profane or obscene language changes school culture and builds student defiance.

During the lunch period, a student arrives at my locked classroom door. She bangs on the door several times and says, *"you better stop fucking calling my mother and telling her lies."*

Cursing has become more common in society, and regrettably, curse words are now in the schoolhouse as well. Given the lack of frontal lobe development in students, they may choose profanity to exert power, impress their peers, seek attention, and spread emotional chaos. Depending on school culture, certain words or phrases frequently echo in school hallways.

School Culture and Climate

We think of school culture as norms, values, and beliefs that unite and shape any school environment. Cultures are influenced by both patterns and practices in the schoolhouse, and by parents, communities, and the social- economic environment of schools. Moreover, the design of our social environment advances social evolutions that include new attitudes and behaviors that in turn affect cultural attitudes and behaviors in the schoolhouse. Harmful cultural elements associated with our social evolution seep into the schoolhouse, and teachers are the first individuals to experience the impact.

Like most professionals working in an environment with decorum, teachers utilize language for optimal communication with colleagues and clients. However, significant changes in social culture invite students to freely curse at teachers, walk out of classrooms, verbally threaten teachers, and blatantly lie about what happens in a teacher's classroom with or without the support of social media. Student actions are followed by parents who believe only what their children say about teachers and passionately believe a hierarchical process for complaining about teachers or student grades does not exist. When parents transfer antisocial behaviors to the schoolhouse, the process reinforces disrespect toward educators.

Changes in school culture link to evolving social changes, and once these changes enter the schoolhouse, the influence on a teacher's ability to control the classroom environment, teach effectively, and remain mentally well are challenged.

In the 1980s, I taught in Washington, DC, as the city experienced extreme levels of drug-related violence. I dodged bullets, stepped over dead bodies to get in my car, taught 15-year-old drug dealers, knew students who were murderers, witnessed students who were shot while standing next to me, and experienced the loss of countless former students. In my teaching career, this was my first significant stressor. These experiences changed my persona, and I removed the emotional attachment of teaching to survive.

While I gradually returned some of my emotional attachment toward students, I remain guarded.

As one would expect, new challenges are entering the schoolhouse each school year, and the new challenges are violent—and directed toward anyone in a school. On April 20, 1999, a new realism materialized in school culture when two teenage students carrying guns and bombs walked into Columbine High School, and 13 people, including themselves and one teacher, were killed. The gun violence at Columbine was not the first school shooting but indeed an event that changed school culture throughout the United States.

Schools practice "death drills," a type of emergency training, four times during the school year using various scenarios associated with violence. There are security officers in schools and a list of rules and policies developed to enhance security, and classroom doors always remain locked. There are direct call buttons to the central office and a telephone in most classrooms, but nothing can directly protect teachers from violence and harassment in their classroom. In most school districts, student safety is paramount while ignoring teacher victimization. With changes in school culture, a teacher's professional environment now includes teacher victimizations, new antisocial behaviors, incivility, and schoolhouse conflicts.

Teacher Victimization

One of the most underreported topics, the victimization of teachers, seldom makes local news coverage. It is more probable to hear about student victimization, especially child sexual abuse. Teacher victimization happens in both elementary and secondary schools nationwide, regardless of a school's location or social-economic environment. However, the study of violence toward teachers is new, and some scholars believe research in this area only began in the past 10 years.

During the 2015-16 school year, 10 percent of teachers reported threats with injury by a student in their public school, and 6 percent of teachers reported being physically attacked by one of their students. Public schools reported at least one serious disciplinary action for specific offenses (Musu-Gillette et al., 2018). At the same time, some scholars believe that nationwide, 80 percent of teachers experience at least one act of victimization within a school year.

In a smaller national survey of approximately 5,000 teachers, conducted by the American Psychological Association's Task Force on Violence Against Teachers (2016), the research found that 37 percent of teachers were the target of obscene or sexual remarks from students, 31 percent experienced obscene gestures or were groped by students, and 27 percent reported receiving verbal threats from students. In the same survey, according to Dr. Dorothy Eselage, the data did not differ because of the school setting, gender, or years of teaching. In fact, according to DeVoe et al., 2003, 1.3 million nonfatal crimes (including 473,000 violent crimes) were committed against America's teachers from 1997 through 2001.

The more students verbally use curse words in everyday dialogue, the more these words influence school culture. From the schoolhouse to the school bus to classrooms and hallways to verbally abusing teachers, there is an increase in verbal abuse, which is a form of mental abuse and bullying. Local school districts have implemented "no tolerance for bullying" and "bully-free zones" to protect students. Teachers are trained to recognize signs of student bullying and how to prevent bullying in school communities. However, there are thousands of cases reported about students bullying and intimidating teachers about grades, enforcing discipline, and just personal dislike of individual teachers. These cases involve both students and parents at all school levels.

Two young ladies arrive at my classroom door, which is locked, and peer through the glass window. "There she is...she had a sexual change operation...she use to be a man...I wonder who fucks that bitch." Unaware that I could hear their conversation, or they did not care, the lack of civility eludes them.

The nature of teacher victimization broadens when students purposely disturb classrooms with bad behaviors. These behaviors include purposely talking out loud while the teacher gives directions, watching videos on cell phones, and engaging other students to watch, or merely cursing at teachers and walking out the classroom. Acts of intimidation occur in hallways where students are emboldened to physically bump teachers or force teachers to walk around their hostile stakeout in a hallway.

"...was extremely disruptive in his 4th period class... demanding that he leave the classroom before members of the football team were called for early dismissal...he showed no interest in getting his Google Classroom code or assignments...he came to class without any materials (notebook/pens)..."

"The student walked out of class at 3:30 p.m. ...was rude and disruptive during class...refused to stop talking while I was introducing the lesson...spoke to her mother this afternoon and her mother has scheduled a meeting with me Monday..."

"...walked out of class at 1:35 p.m. ...disrupted the entire class period (talking to me while giving directions/notes) ...there are no working phone numbers to contact her mother..."

"...during class, the student contacted her mother on her cell phone and proceeded to talk to mother while I was introducing the lesson...I asked the student several times to put the phone away...the student than indicated that her mother wanted to talk to me, but I refused."

Disruptive behaviors require time to speak with troublesome students about their behaviors, contact parents, and administrative follow-up with paperwork. All of that time takes away from engaging with students and lesson planning while adding to a teacher's daily stress and frustration. Experienced teachers choose their battles and can implement a plan from their repertoire that provides recovery. For new teachers, without mentors and administrative support, disruptive students can lead to early burnout and choosing another profession.

Increasingly teachers are becoming victims of cyberbullying. In a recent survey of tens of thousands of teachers, one in seven teachers reported being cyberbullied, 68 percent said they received unpleasant emails, 26 percent said they are subjected to abuse on websites, and 28 percent said they received abusive text messages (National Teacher and Principal Survey, 2019). Bullying of teachers comes from both students and parents, and parents are going so far as to use "GroupMe" to post negative reviews about teachers. In addition, some parents use student emails to evaluate a teacher's response and to deceive teachers. Increasingly teacher bullying becomes a social norm practiced by both parents and students.

Parent and Administrative Bullying

Parents are not afraid of using phone calls, social media, or emails to bully teachers, or demand parent conferences to support their child's defiant and disruptive behaviors. This type of teacher victimization perpetuates a culture of disrespecting teachers. Naturally, if students witness parent disrespect toward teachers, students are encouraged to extend the disrespect in a teacher's classroom.

Every parent has the right to support their child. However, in the era of teacher victimization, students are increasingly fabricating scenarios, and parents are more willing to believe what is conveyed by their students. So often, the hierarchical process for parent grievances is dismissed by parents who believe that contacting school administrators, before any informal or formal meeting with a teacher, provides the immediate and desired outcome.

Parent One

`"I am requesting an immediate Cease and Desist be made regarding the disparaging treatment....is being` subjected to in... class and that she be provided with the information required to make up the missing assignment with the same information, study material, notes, etc. the other students had available at the time of the assignment. I am also requesting a copy of the assignment after it has been graded."

Parent Two

"If my request is not meant I will be contacting the regional office and submitting a formal written complaint regarding these subtle but not subtle incidents that keep reoccurring. There appears to be some underlying ulterior motives lingering in the air and it's impacting my daughters spirit, attacking her character, and impacting her GPA as an aspiring college student. IT NEEDS TO STOP!!!"

Parent Three

"Dear ...
I am submitting this letter as a formal complaint to address a number of serious concerns related to the teaching and grading practices of... Once you have reviewed these concerns below, you will understand why we are disputing the legitimacy of our daughter, grade. In addition, we are requesting a change of grade pending a full audit of how her grades were assessed, issued, and calculated.

Please be advised that this complaint letter is not an attack on ...character or integrity. It is simply to address these ongoing concerns which appear to be affecting our daughter's academic performance and morale, as well as those of her peers and other students who are enrolled in her class.

That being said, we do not want ... to suffer a backlash for being a whistle blower or bringing this to our attention as we are doing so with you. For some reason unbeknownst to her, she believes that... "does not like her" because she is constantly and tactfully inquiring about grades that appear to be ambiguous, missing, extremely low and/or recorded late.

Specifically, the issues with...teaching and grading practices as follows:

- *Has never returned back graded assignments to her students with the exception of one essay which was an autobiographical sketch about her life story.*

- *Fails to provide comments and/or areas for improvement related to graded assignments.*

- *Frequently claims to loose, misplace or never have received submitted assignments.*

- *Solicited favors from our daughter with the promise of extra credit without actual issuing points as mutually agreed.*

- *Consistently assigns 50 item tests with a 35-40 minute time frame to complete in a subject matter that requires focus and concentration.*

- *Does not review tests or provide feedback to reinforce learning.*

- *Consistently assigns random tests without teaching material to students.*

- *Reportedly uses gradecam website to grade scantrons which is subject to technical error.*

- *Assigns identical grades to multiple students for the same test.*

- *Fails to enter grades via ... in a timely manner.*

- *Does not spend adequate time teaching or engaging with students about material but appears to be consumed with work that needs to be completed at her desk.*

- *Always directs students to her website without answering their questions and/or addressing their concerns.*

- *Avoided meeting and/or acknowledging parents waiting to meet with her on two separate occasions during Parent Teacher conference by allowing time to run out.*

- *Talks to students in a demeaning manner which impacts student morale and creates an unproductive learning environment.*

- *Although I brought most of these issues to... attention by phone, it appears that the matter has not improved but has gotten worse. As a college educator and consultant, I commended...in her effort to introduce students to independent learning as they prepare to enter college. However, it appears that her strategy for grading and assessments coupled with her teaching practices or lack thereof is a burden that she does not appear to want to be bothered with.*

- *As such, my husband and I do not believe the grades are valid and therefore extremely biased. It is important to note that our daughter is an honor roll student who loves learning and is extremely obsessed with her grades. She has high expectations of herself and from her teachers. What parent, teacher or administrator can fault a child with the insight to know that something is wrong with this picture?*

- *It is our sincerest hope that you can help us find a favorable resolution to this matter so our daughter's grades, including her peers, are accurate, unbiased or retaliatory. If you have any questions, comments or concerns, please feel free to contact me on my cell phone at... or home at... to discuss this matter."*

    Cc: Teacher, Principal, Instructional Director

Parent Four

"...refused to grade my daughter's homework assignment...my daughter showed me the assignment and I saw her complete the assignment..."

A Teacher's Comment to a Colleague

"Why are parents experts about what happens in my classroom according to their child...the student indicated that I refused to grade her homework...at the "parent conference" the student admitted she walked out of class before submitting the assignment... according to the student, she had somewhere to go... the student lied to her mother, demanded that her mother schedule a parent/teacher conference and than changed her actuations...neither the mother or the daughter apologized for the lie... the mother just wanted me to accept the assignment, but I refused..."

Parent Five

"Since the parent meeting I had with you on..., I have some additional concerns that have surfaced as a result of me having discussions with my daughter....

Last week during class...raised her hand to ask you a question as to when are you planning to collect assignments that have been completed so they can be graded and receive credit for ...stated to me that she did not communicate the question to you in a disrespectful way but your response was unkind and not warranted. Is there a reason why you would respond in a manner that is upsetting if the student is asking you a question in a respectful manner?

During class today...stated you explained work they were doing in class but only explained it one time. When asked by the majority of the class to explain the work again due to the class not understanding, your response was that you would not explain it again. ... said it was not until you instructed students to turn in their papers and from that point is when you explained the work again. I am not sure how this helps the class to understand what you are teaching and expect the class to follow along if their papers were collected.

As a parent I want... to be comfortable in a learning environment where the respect is given on both sides and assistance/clarification is provided if needed when she does not understand and needs further instruction."

Teacher's Response

"The classroom situation you described did not occur nor did I explain an assignment once, before the assessment...the assessment, at the end of the class period, was based on re-teaching the topic for reinforcement and students were allowed to use their notes and the notes posted on the classroom board. You may want to encourage... to put her cell phone away and devote all her attention to class activities and ask questions for clarity. Staying on her cell phone during class is a major distraction. I invite you to visit the classroom."

The results from a 2018 Harris Poll revealed that only 31 percent of Americans believe students respect teachers, almost half of Americans believe parents respect teachers (49 percent), and 61 percent of parents believe teachers respect students, a decline from previous years as well as an alarming trend. Interestingly, individuals polled believed that only 58 percent of administrators respect teachers.

Administrative bullying to remove a teacher often starts with violation of union rules as some administrators assume teachers are unaware of their employee rights. Administrators may begin interrupting a teacher's classroom by pulling out students one-by-one to talk and telling students not to share their conversations with the teacher. Bullying teachers with accusations when there is no evidence to support the accusation, and requiring teachers to address an administrator's or parent's concern continues in most school districts.

According to Long (2012), a teacher in Augusta, Maine, left her job after her health began to deteriorate from administrative bullying. She was accused of not using technology in the classroom, even though all her students were assigned laptops and required to use computers based on the curriculum. The same administrator criticized the teacher for receiving support from a literacy mentor when several of her students needed support. Finally, the teacher was placed on a behavior modification plan and forced to submit her lesson plans one week in advance for administrative approval.

Combine administrative bullying with a baseless accusation, often initiated by parents, and teachers in public education are encouraged to walk away from the profession. Teacher support is essential, especially for new teachers, and at all stages of the teaching profession. Teachers need administrative support for a variety of reasons, but especially to be effective when managing student behaviors.

The very nature of public education requires that teachers embrace and implement a variety of tasks. The following is an example of a classroom teacher job description:

- Work is performed under the supervision of the principal.

- Plan, prepare, and deliver lesson plans and instructional materials that facilitate active learning.

- Develops schemes of work, lesson plans, and tests that are in accordance with established procedures.

- Instruct and monitor students in the use of learning materials and equipment.

- Use relevant technology to support and differentiate instruction.

- Manage student behavior in the classroom by establishing and enforcing rules and procedures.

- Maintain discipline in accordance with the rules and disciplinary systems of the school.

- Provide appropriate feedback on work.

- Encourage and monitor the progress of individual students and use information to adjust teaching strategies.

- Maintain accurate and complete records of students' progress and development.

- Update all necessary records accurately and completely as required by laws, district policies, and school regulations.

- Prepare required reports on students and activities.

- Participate in department, school, district and parent meetings.

- Communicate necessary information regularly to students, colleagues, and parents regarding student progress and student needs.

- Establish and communicate clear objectives for all learning activities.

- Prepare classroom for class activities.

- Provide a variety of learning materials and resources for use in educational activities.

- Observe and evaluate students' performance and development.

- Assign and grade classwork, homework, tests, and assignments.

- Demonstrate preparation and skill in working with students from diverse cultural, economic, and ability backgrounds.

- Encourage parent and community involvement, obtain information for parents when requested, promptly return phone calls, and answer emails.

- Participate in appropriate professional activities.

- Participate in extracurricular activities such as social activities, sporting activities, clubs, and student organizations as directed.

- To perform this job successfully, an individual must be able to perform each essential duty satisfactorily.

- The requirements are representative of the knowledge, skill, and/or ability required.

- Reasonable accommodations may be made to enable individuals with disabilities to perform the essential functions.

- Together with the Learning Support Assistants, developing and implementing the Individual Educational Program (IEP) of students with Individual Educational Needs and participating in IEP and Individual Transition Plan (ITP) meetings

- B.A/B. S degree in teaching from an accredited institution or related field teaching.

- A certification in teaching in appropriate subject area.

- Ability to establish and maintain cooperative and effective working relationships with others.

- Ability to communicate effectively orally and in writing.

- Must have the ability and proven ability to report to work on a regular and punctual basis.

- Perform all other related work delegated or required to accomplish the objectives of the total school program.

- Knowledge of and ability to implement relevant technology.

- Meet professional teacher education requirements of school, district, and state.

- Physical requirements: regularly required to sit, stand, walk, talk, hear, operate a computer, hand-held learning devices and other office equipment, reach with hands and arms, and must occasionally lift and/or move up to 10 pounds.

Documenting a teacher's shortcomings, stalking their classroom, creating paper trails with accusations, and assuming these elements will force teachers out the classroom is cruel and can lead to teacher-generated lawsuits. At the same time, when teachers are not productive, most school districts have administrative and disciplinary policies for principals to follow — but choosing to circumvent established school district policies can create a hostile working environment for all teachers and support staff.

In 2017 a teacher's recommendations for dealing with workplace bullying in school led to a six-figure payout after the teacher was bullied by the school principal. In this case, a collaborative staff culture changed with the arrival of a new principal who created a toxic environment. Toxic work environments can lead to teachers getting sick, a decline in their immune system, nightmares, and suffering from anxiety (Singhal, 2017).

A lack of interpersonal and organizational factors can escalate bullying. By contrast, when principals communicate with teachers and help them to succeed, principals can erode mistrust and create a more dynamic environment by providing consistent feedback over time and tangible support to assist teachers with improving (Fagell, 2018).

Administrator One

"During the school year I have received an excessive amount of calls and emails from parents with complaints regarding their child being in your class. In my conversations with parents their concerns are 1. Your teaching methods- students tell their parents that you don't teach- the class consists of all writing down notes from the textbook- you are accused of not providing any assistance or instruction. 2. not entering

2 grades per week. 3. not responding to parent requests, emails, within 48 hours. Many parents have set up parent teacher conferences and are still unsatisfied with your classroom and would prefer a class change. With so many negative perceptions, or feedback from parents and students it is enormously challenging for students to remain optimistic or engaged. There are serious allegations and concerns that I believe require some courageous conversations between all stakeholders. Let the process begin, now."

Administrator Two

"I am receiving a large amount of complaints from students and parents concerning a variety of issues...ie. teacher not providng checks on class assignments...notebook checks...classroom assistance with lesson expectations...communication with students during lesson ie. questions. Assistance...help...mutual respect . Courtesy...perhaps you need to see me. ....

THANKS"

Administrator Three (Sent to all staff members)

"As I watch the news tonight and hear stories from high school students and staff members in Florida I'm so incredibly saddened by the fact that schools continue to be a target for violence. In the coming hours and days I'm sure we will learn more about what was behind this horrific incident. From the images and stories I've heard so far it appears that once again educators stood up as heroes and by acting quickly and following school procedures saved the lives of students in their care.

The administrative team and security team will meet to review school safety procedures and protocols. Please be prepared for some of our students to be impacted by this school shooting. While some students may want to speak about it for others the best thing will be to have a normal school day and be reassured that they are safe at .... Please use your best professional judgement.

Please note that a hashtag has been set up on twitter #stonemanshooting and some of our students might be looking at videos that will be uploaded on Twitter using this hashtag.

Any students who seem emotionally impacted by this incident should be sent to the counseling office to be assessed.

To help guide you in how you should support students tomorrow I've provided a link to an article from the NEA and pasted some relevant sections of the article below. The article has several additional resources linked at the bottom.

I've also pasted the directions for a lock down drill at the bottom of this email in case you would like to review it with students. I realize we recently conducted a lock down drill but it may help to reassure students and remind them of the safety protocols we have in place.

As always, if you have safety concerns about any of our students please share that information with the appropriate grade level administrator. Students who speak about violence or guns should be referred to their administrators so that if there is a serious problem they can get help."

Teacher Response to Administrator Three (Sent to all members of the staff)

"What about the teachers...what about us...you mention students 11 times...what about our stress and the desire to survive each day...what about us?"

Administrator Three Response (Sent to all members of the staff)

"As adults, we have had a myriad of life experiences that have prepared us to accept, address, and deal with the tragedies that occur not only in our personal lives; but in the world we live in. Many of our students have not had those experiences at their young age and as educators we should assist them in trying to process these tragedies so they can make sense of what has happened. If any adult needs support, please feel free to see me for assistance."

Administrator Four

"It was brought to the attention of ... and myself that the parent of ... received court documents from your attorney suing her for defamation of character, etc (Mrs. ... actually made a complaint to Ms. ... via a telephone conversation). Her specific complaint was the court documents arrived via mail and she was not served and she is concerned that you utilized ... in order to obtain her personal information in order to have the document mailed to her home. I wanted to ensure that you were aware of the concern and take the opportunity to mention ... and ... which focuses on the confidential use of student information for school related purposes only. I am not sure of the specifics of the documents she received and how she received them, but I wanted to make you aware. Thank you in advance."

In addition to administrative bullying, teacher computers are hacked, sent viruses, and in some cases, a teacher's posted assignments on virtual learning environments are deleted. The response to teacher cyberbullying by school districts varies even though bullying occurs in small rural school districts as well as large suburban and urban school districts. School districts seldom offer legal support to teachers and some school districts provide no directives for reporting cyberbullying. Teachers can reach out to their union or hire their own lawyer.

Overall, the issue of teacher victimization is not limited to the United States, this is a global issue. In Canada, student bullying of teachers has reached epidemic proportions.

Teachers are bullied in various ways, such as students acting out in the class, challenging the teacher, and spreading rumors using social media to cyberbully teachers (Riggio, 2017). In the United Kingdom, one study reported that 42 percent of teachers were being assaulted or harassed by students on the web and 60 percent of students between the ages of 11 and 16 years old have bullied a teacher. England's University of Plymouth released a research study indicating that one-quarter of teachers surveyed suffered abuse that was generated by parents (BBC News, 2011).

When faced with accusations that are racist, sexist, and homophobic, teachers often choose to resign given that defamatory allegations require proof of increasing hatred toward the individual teacher. A recent National Public Radio story reported that a teacher in North Carolina resigned after students in his 10th grade English class created a parody Twitter account in his name portraying him as a drug addict, violent person, and super sexual (Yoshida, 2013). Schools begin each year with a review of policies and procedures, but a far greater emphasis is placed on policies related to students than teachers.

In cases where the teacher is stalked, harassed, or received physical and sexual threats, the police must be involved as these are criminal offenses. The biggest challenge is identifying who issued the threat. In England, The Education and Inspections Act of 2006 grants school staff the right to confiscate a mobile phone that is used to disturb a class, but school staff cannot search the content of a phone without the student's consent. Globally, most public schools review cyberbullying policies outlined in student handbooks; however, so far, cyberbullying toward teachers is increasing.

Marijuana in the Schoolhouse

Imagine walking into a school and you smell marijuana. Imagine you smell marijuana every day you enter a school. This is common for educators given that marijuana is the most commonly used substance by adolescents after alcohol. While the use of marijuana is more common among older adolescents, 5 percent of 8th grade students, 14 percent of 10th grade students, 23 percent of 12th grade students, and 22 percent of college students reported using marijuana at least once in the past month in 2016 (Johnston et al., 2017). In a recent search for data on teenagers smoking marijuana in schools and the impact on teachers, there is nothing that speaks to this topic. You are more likely to find information on drug resources for educators to instruct students about the use of drugs, cannabis use, and parents and drug use. The exposure to second-hand marijuana smoke can cause itchiness, rashes, skin irritations, and mild allergic reactions. The smoking of marijuana in workplace spaces, including schools, is a hazard. However, depending on marijuana laws in a school district, possession and the amount of marijuana found on a student, the ability to arrest students for selling and using marijuana on school grounds varies. Laws do not prevent the victimization of an educator's health in their workplace.

"Sadly, I'm accustomed to the smell of marijuana in the school and a student walks by reeking of marijuana while I'm sitting in the hall and reviewing emails. The second-hand ingestion causes my chest to hurt, my heart rate increases, and I am not feeling well. At the same time, I read a message from the principal about a last-minute professional development training in the auditorium. I indicate to the principal that I am ill resulting from second-hand marijuana and after seeing the school nurse, I will not attend the professional development. The principal emailed me and firmly states that he plans to write a disciplinary action since I did not attend the professional development session."

Sexually Assaulting Teachers

A recent search for research data about teachers who are sexually assaulted at work yielded absolutely nothing. Sexual assaults on teachers are rolled into data about obscene or sexual remarks from students. According Lucas (2019), extremely limited research related to violence against teachers exists and the research available contradicts official statistics. Teachers are dissuaded from reporting incidents of violence.

Public schools in Argentina experienced an increase in violence against teachers and the government passed a law classifying attacks on teachers as an aggravated assault. Attempts to introduce similar laws in the United States were quickly criticized for creating a fast-track from school to prison. However, the cost of teacher victimization affects teachers, parents, and taxpayers, and in the United States exceeds 2 billion dollars annually (Lucas, 2019).

"I asked him to wait at the classroom door, however, he followed me into the classroom and proceeded to gyrate behind me. My fight or flight reaction forced me to rotate with my wrist ready to encounter contact. Given that I have never been in a fight and if you hit me, I would have a heart attack and die. A student in the classroom responds, 'what are you doing?'...I share the incident with my husband that evening and I'm

crying...the next day my husband and I spoke with the principal about the incident and I return home to recover."

"It is the second time she touched me but the last time she touched my hips as I walked by her desk. I report the incident, meet with the student, her mother, and school counselor. The mother comments, "I told you to stop doing this to teachers." No one files a sexual harassment report."

There is a rise in the number of cases of sexual misconduct and teacher/student relationships due to the use of social media and cell phones. In 2015, Anderson & Jiang indicated that 80 percent of children age 12-17 had a cell phone and 94 percent had a Facebook account. In 2014, The Washington Post stated that 35 percent of educators convicted or accused of sexual misconduct used social media to establish and/or continue their student relationships. It is ironic that the seriousness of sexual assaults on teachers is not a major concern given that sexual harassment in the workplace is a major issue. Violence against teachers remains a silent crisis.

Overall, teachers who are affected by victimization lose their confidence and often experience a reduced desire to teach at a higher standard that may challenge students, and thus increase the probability of retaliation from students and parents. As teachers are increasingly victimized, they are likely to lose their love for the profession, particularly if school districts and teacher unions do not have the power to stop teacher victimization, implement policies that strongly protect teachers, and take legal actions to support teachers who are victimized. With increasing teacher shortages nationwide, a profession without mandatory guidelines to protect its members will continue to see fewer and fewer individuals entering the profession.

6 PUBLIC EDUCATION AND BLACK CHILDREN

No Need to Educate Black Children

Structural racism prohibits Blacks from receiving an education in public schools. Society saw no reason to educate Blacks just to pick cotton or to enter slavery by another name: sharecropping. When public education aligned with the economic profits of farming, Black children in rural areas barely needed to read or sign their names. When segregated high schools for Blacks were established, institutional racism and policies prevented Blacks from obtaining jobs in the federal government other than in low wage jobs such as cooks, chauffeurs, or elevator operators. In the 1970s, Black men with master's degrees and doctoral degrees had to settle for jobs in the United States Post Office to feed their families.

In 1917, a Federal Government survey titled Negro Education (two volumes) implied that Blacks were preordained to specific roles in society and thus, they did not need to be educated beyond their destinations as servants, blacksmiths, and farmhands. Negro Education did suggest that while the education of Blacks in the South was indeed a problem, the solution was public policy and philanthropic funding. The report criticized Black educators and parents who insisted on pre- collegiate education for Black children and instead defined the appropriate education for Black children to include technical education, instruction in hygiene, manual training, and agricultural education.

According to the survey, too many colleges and universities were a waste of money and time for Black children, and indeed dual (segregated) school systems, while an economic burden especially for southern states, were in some ways wasteful and inefficient as well as ill-equipped and filthy. The survey proposed a different curriculum for Black schools, a belief supported by southern groups who believed that economic and psychological differences between Blacks and whites necessitated different methods of teaching. Believing that Black parents were not knowledgeable about education and out of touch with progressive education, the survey recommended that an education aligned with industrial pursuits would be most appropriate. With over 50 percent of the Negro population in "Black belt counties" during the early 1900s, inequalities between the expenditures for white and Colored schools were well established and institutional racism and policies supported the belief that there was no need to educate Blacks (Negro Education, 1917).

Naturally, Black leaders responded, especially W.E.B. Du Bois, who viewed the survey as dangerous because it implied that Black private schools in the South must cooperate with southern whites and that Black colleges should willingly accept control by state education boards and northern foundations. As editor of the July 1918 National Association for the Advancement of Colored People (NAACP) magazine, The Crisis, Du Bois continued his attack on the Negro Education survey. Du Bois believed that increased control over Black education would restrict Black students to learning only the skills aligned with laborers and servants. Thus, the July issue in 1918, dedicated to education, listed 74 Black college graduates and their pictures.

Psychologists, Drs. Kenneth Clark and his wife Mamie Phipps Clark believed that Black children were systemically deprived of education with rigorous standards and only exposed to low-academic standards in segregated public schools. Raised in Harlem, New York, Dr. Kenneth Clark described Harlem segregated public schools as inefficient, inferior, and deteriorating. The majority of white teachers were substituting, inexperienced, and could not effectively discipline students in the classroom. Moreover, white teachers held lower expectations for Black students and accepted substandard performances from students based on the belief that Black students living in working class communities did not need exposure to rigorous standards. Harlem's segregated school environment assumed Black students had low intellectual levels as well, a process that Dr. Kenneth Clark described as creating rigid and intolerable pathology, injustice, and supporting racism (Harlem World Magazine, 2018).

By the twentieth century, America's previously established history of institutional racism continued to endorse, reinforce, and aggressively create policies supported by federal, state, and local governments to maintain segregation. The very agents that supported segregation were now the ones in charge of transitioning to desegregated public schools. As might be expected, the transition did not come with a set of plans designed to incorporate the sociocultural idiosyncrasies of Black children, a timeframe, a plan to incorporate the opinions of Black parents when establishing educational policies or ensuring that local governments and school districts would not retaliate by implementing new race-based policies. Instead, the Southern Manifesto (1956), representing southern defiance against *Brown* and signed by 82 U.S. Representatives and 19 U.S. Senators (all from former Confederate states), believed that *Brown* abused judicial power and encroached on states' rights. Southern states were urged to create new laws to resist school desegregation (Southern Manifesto, 1956). However, the practice of resisting the implementation of *Brown* was not exclusive to southern states. States in the north as well as the south used race-based public policies to practice residential segregation and thus control and still resist the desegregation of public schools. Even with the intent to enforce the *Browns (I and II)*, residential segregation and socioeconomic stratification still restricted academic achievement and increased disparities, especially in hypersegregated Black enclaves. Thus, as housing discrimination became more institutionalized, the option of transitioning to middle-class communities and better school districts did not exist for Blacks and other ethnic groups of color.

Housing Segregation

Historically, government policies have segregated the nation's housing and directed housing segregation primarily at Black working and middle-class parents with children. Black families were placed into permanently segregated enclaves for decades as government policies continuously added layers that contributed to social isolation and economic disparities. By denying job opportunities and economic stability, endorsing racially separate public housing in cities, using exclusion zoning laws in the suburbs and restrictive covenants that prohibited selling homes to Blacks, more and more Blacks were disproportionately forced to live in economically deprived communities—communities that did not receive school funding equality, essential educational opportunities, and social components to support the needs of Black children. Even with school desegregation attempts, race-based policies were used to block permanent desegregation of public schools through segregated housing.

In 1935, the Federal Housing Authority's (FHA's) Underwriting Manual instructed realtors that for neighborhoods to retain stability, the same social and racial classes needed to occupy neighborhoods. The FHA preferred mortgages where boulevards and highways provided natural barriers to separate Black and white families and thus, protect white neighborhoods from adverse influences (Rothstein, 2017). This position is like Dr. Kenneth Clark's assertion that Black ghettos had an invisible wall that marked physical terrain for poverty and exclusion (Clark, 1967).

The FHA manual also stated that home mortgages in communities where students from a lower level of society or an incompatible race interact, created neighborhoods that are less stable and made mortgage lending risky. Consistently, the FHA would not guarantee mortgages to Blacks or whites who might lease to Blacks, regardless of creditworthiness. The U.S. Commission on Civil Rights in 1973 concluded that both the housing industry and the federal government established the legacy of segregated housing and a system of residential segregation (Rothstein, 2017). With the use of institutional racism, both government policies and local school board policies implemented attendance boundaries to separate Black and white students and deny opportunities to Black families. Ultimately, political and economic institutions created and enforced policies that segregated people of color in housing, income, and education.

Renting and Segregation

For economic stability, low-income families depend on affordable rental housing, but the severe shortage of affordable rental homes increases the probability of being homeless. Low-income renters with incomes at or below the poverty level faced a shortage of more than 7.2 million affordable and available rental homes in 2019. Renters who spend more than half of their income on housing have less income for other necessities like food and medical care (National Low Income Housing Coalition, 2019). Recent federal policies (under the Donald Trump Administration) reduced federal housing assistance for the lowest income households, increased rents, and changed employment requirements. Changes made in 2017 denied three out of four low-income households housing assistance. Without question, stable housing provides positive economic, educational, and health outcomes for struggling families. The lack of stable housing affects student learning and decreases academic achievement (Brennan et al., 2014).

Extremely low-income renters who have children are more likely to be financially burdened and severe housing cost contributes to a deterioration in household members' physical and mental well-being, reduces health care spending by 75 percent, and spending for food by 40 percent (Joint Center for Housing Studies, 2017). Like severe housing costs, financial hardships are linked with an individual's psychological well-being (Maqbool et al., 2015). Overall, 35 percent of Black and 29 percent of Hispanic renter households experience extremely low incomes. White renter households make up 21 percent of deficient-income individuals. In general, white renters receive higher wages and are less likely to experience disparities in income and wealth (National Low Income Housing Coalition, 2019).

Continuous housing segregation creates ethnic enclaves with real economic disadvantages. With a shortage of available housing and few homes available to families in diverse communities, Blacks pay higher rents and home prices in Black neighborhoods than whites in predominantly white neighborhoods. This type of economic disadvantage forces Blacks to use their disposable income toward higher rents and housing cost, which reduces their chances of saving to buy a home in a middle-class neighborhood. In addition, when commuting from urban areas to jobs located in suburban areas, transportation cost is another obstacle. All these components formulated by race-based policies and generated by governments impact income, residence, and school choices (Rothstein, 2017).

Housing segregation traps Black families and their school-age children in environments where public schools can only provide educational disadvantages that eventually limit student abilities to merge into middle-class workplaces. In the 1980s, especially 1988, nearly 50 percent of Black students attended ethnic majority schools. In 2019, Black and Hispanic students were far more likely to attend the same ethnic schools in high-poverty neighborhoods, and in low-achieving school districts (Logan et al., 2017). The issue is not that Black and Hispanic students need white students to be successful in school. Instead, the issue is that segregated schools are devoid of academic resources, promote educational stratification, and deny children of color opportunities to build social capital and obtain skills related to the future of work. These are the very skills that can assure life-sustaining employment and overall well-being in a global economy.

Fast forward to 2019, where the most disadvantaged Black and Hispanic children attend schools in resegregated neighborhoods with pronounced disparities in communities segregated by race and class. Addressing only educational inequalities without addressing economic inequalities between racial groups increases segregation during a period of profound economic and demographic changes occurring in American society.

Economic Disparities

Some scholars state that Black Americans were never meant to achieve equality in education or wealth given that laws have continuously segregated opportunities to receive an education and thus, income equality. From the Thirteenth Amendment, Jim Crow laws, lynching, exclusion from the Social Security Act, exclusion within the G.I. Bill of Rights in southern states, neighborhood segregation, public school segregation, voting rights, and housing discrimination policies are all inequalities that oppress and limit education and economic opportunities for people of color. Even social program eligibility historically prohibits low-income families from accumulating wealth and saving for economic hardships. The Temporary Assistance for Needy Families program (TANF) and the Supplemental Nutrition Assistance Program (SNAP), depending on which state families live, limit the amount of money you can have in a savings account. For those who own a car, there is a limit on the value of the car you can own. By contrast, asset accumulation for higher-income families is rewarded with tax incentives such as home mortgage interest deduction, retirement accounts, college saving plans, and medical saving accounts (Pirog, 2017).

The causes for racial wealth gaps continue in the form of tax cuts. President Trump's 2017 Tax Cut and Jobs Act gives families earning $25,000 or less per year a $40 tax cut and those earning over $3 million annually, a $940,000 tax break. This type of tax cut widens the wealth gap (Amedeo, 2019). Without a raise in the minimum wage, individuals are more likely to be a part of the working poor with no expendable income to build wealth or to become homeowners. Cities that increase the minimum wage reduce poverty and the reliance on government programs (Amedeo, 2019).

As America's affluent families increased their net worth, individuals at the bottom moved into negative wealth where their debts exceed their assets. The median family income for Latino families increased between 1983 and 2016. Black family median income decreased from $7,323 in 1983 to $3,557 in 2016. However, the median white family income is 41 times higher than the Black family median income and 22 times more than Latino family median income. White family median income in 1983 was slightly over $110,000 and in 2016 nearly $147,000. Overall, America's economic system unfairly favors powerful interests (Institute for Policy Studies, 2019).

Along racial lines, according to the Economic Policy Institute, 25 percent of Black families are extremely poor and have a negative net worth. As a result, the poorest families decrease the average wealth of all Blacks. Ironically, the wealth gap exists among Blacks with advanced degrees and two-parent homes. Individuals of color with professional degrees have $200,000 less in wealth compared to their white counterparts and in some cases, wealth for Black and Hispanic college graduates is less than white high school dropouts. Just the same, two-parent Black households have less wealth than single-parent white households (Amedeo, 2019).

The combination of economic inequality, housing segregation and gentrification, and America's increasing wealth gap removes more and more families of color from existing in middle-class communities and their children from attending public schools that receive stable financial support and resources directly linked to academic achievement and positive educational outcomes. An increasing wealth gap between white families and families of color supports privilege and allows wealthy and predominately white public school districts to receive substantial school financial support that is based on property taxes. This financial support is isolated in communities created by racialized perceptions of good communities and schools.

It is only natural that a major reduction in financial support for education resources, including qualified teachers, produces lower academic outcomes. Armed with standardized testing results to indicate a growing achievement gap between white students and students of color, there is justification to provide less and less monies to resegregated school districts with populations where students of color are the majority. But understand that this process is not about widening achievement gaps but the deliberate proliferation of the opportunity gap between white students and students of color—a gap that disqualifies students of color from obtaining life-sustaining employment skills, economic stability, and overall well-being in a highly competitive global society.

The very nature of structural racism analysis speaks to the historical, cultural, and social psychological aspects of America's racialized society. The historical removal of equality in education, cultural resegregation, and the long-term social psychological impact of racism are more evident today and question the need to educate children of color when structural racism infuses a variety of public policies and institutional practices to perpetuate racial group inequity in America's society. In 2020, youth of color (Black and Hispanic) are disproportionately transferred to the juvenile system from their schools and communities. They are disproportionately transferred from juvenile courts to adult courts where they receive a public criminal record and lengthy sentences. At the same time, the nature of structural racism extends to infant mortality, mental health disorders, emotional distress, anxiety, depression, and suicide. Further, students of color with parents who are incarcerated are likely to experience a loss in family income, homelessness, and drop out of school—all elements designed by structural racism.

Resegregation and Social Closure

Resegregation does not present itself as a new tool used by structural racism to continue segregation in housing and education but as a new process for supporting privilege and widening the wealth gap between whites and people of color. Regardless of diversity and integration, resegregation is fostered, supported, and rationalized using racialized perceptions (Wells, 2018). The number of Black and Hispanic students who attend resegregated public schools increases each year at an alarming rate. Black and Hispanic students represent nearly 22 million students in public schools, and they are far more likely to attend schools that are 90-100 percent the same ethnicity. Simultaneously, white and Asian students are increasingly isolated from students of color.

The demographic composition of America's public schools indicates that public elementary and secondary school populations for white students decreased from 61 percent to 49 percent between 2000 and 2015. The percentage of students enrolled in public schools who are white is projected to continue decreasing from 49 to 45 percent between 2015 and 2027 (National Center for Education Statistics, 2019). Between 2000 and 2015, the percentage of Black students also decreased from 17 to 15 percent. In contrast, the percentage of students enrolled in public schools who are Hispanic increased from 16 to 26 percent and Asian/Pacific Islander students increased from 4 to 5 percent during this period. Black students are projected to remain at 15 percent and Hispanic students are projected to increase from 26 percent to 29 percent by 2027 (National Center for Education Statistics, 2019). In Fall 2018, enrollment of public school students (grades pre-kindergarten to 12) was 50.7 million. This enrollment population consisted of 24.1 million students; 7.8 million Black students, 14 million Hispanic students, and 2.6 million Asian students. Pacific Islander, American Indian/Alaska Native, and students identified as two or more races compose 2.3 million students (National Center for Education Statistics, 2019).

Collectively, the student population in public schools nationwide is declining. Students of color are attending schools with fewer white students, the racial composition of school communities varies, and the process for assigning students to schools varies as well. Where possible, school districts can seek racially balanced schools that reflect the community population or school districts can create schools that are predominantly Black and predominantly white. However, reality reflects the fact that more and more school districts are institutionally resegregating students of color as a mode of social closure.

According to Parkin (1979), social closure is a process whereby social collectives maximize rewards by implementing restrictive access to both resources and opportunities for an exceedingly small circle of eligible individuals. The greatest intent of closure is the refusal to share social and economic opportunities with others who have been singled out by any number of group attributes, including race. As Parkin elaborates, this concept, known as exclusionary closure is the attempt of one group to secure a privileged position at the expense of another group, often using power and closure strategies.

The social stratification of Black and Hispanic families when influenced by housing segregation results in majority, isolated, and low-income communities and high-poverty residents. Resegregation contributes to low-achieving schools that are often devoid of basic resources and qualified teachers. Overall, when resegregated schools and predominantly white schools exist within the same school district, an abundance of financial support is allocated to predominately white schools concentrated in higher income communities that reflect higher academic achievement levels. At this point, social stratification and resegregation contribute to developing school status that is associated with and distributed based on a school's racial composition and a community's socioeconomic composition (Logan et al., 2012; Condron & Roscigno, 2003; Clotfelter et al., 2005; Sikkink & Emerson, 2008).

Resegregation is a mode of social exclusion, which causes uneven distribution of resources to schools, increases racial imbalance, and heightens racial isolation and intergroup exposure. Without a substantial and a consistent tax base to fund public schools, low-income communities receive fewer school resources. As a result of white flight, whites leave some school districts with only a handful of students to distribute, and thus racial imbalances occur. But perhaps more important, do school districts with majority students of color need white students to ensure positive outcomes for educational achievement or whether underfunded schools simply distort educational outcomes for students of color and thus, marginalize their abilities to achieve by creating racial bias, cognitive barriers, and ultimately destroying any opportunity to become global citizens? Racial isolation is caused by housing and economic segregation, especially when suburban communities are the overflow for gentrification in major urban cities where whites displace low-income families and rents increase, and when whites create socially constructed strategies to exclude middle-class Blacks from their suburban communities.

In this book, I define race as a social construct and tool used to oppress and control a segment of the population, people of color. By controlling individuals with social, economic, and political restrictions, policies, and laws—whether individually or structurally—we are practicing racism. American society consists of organizations, institutions, and individuals that control, and manufacture policies and laws designed to support inequalities in education, employment, and housing related to people of color. One of the main ways to segregate people of color is with the use of institutional housing policies and practices that have historically determined where people of color can live. The federal government used the National Housing Act of 1934 to advance the migration of whites to suburban communities by offering subsidized home mortgages. The process continued through the 1950s (Kirwan Institute, 2015). Created in the 1930s, the U.S. Property Appraisal System linked property values and eligibility for government loans to race and offered white neighborhoods the highest government property value rating. Government policies especially excluded Blacks from integrating white suburbs. The FHA's manual clearly stated and warned that Blacks were an adverse influence on property values. Thus, by excluding Black families from government-supported housing programs, the perceptions developed that white suburbs were idealistic communities and segregated Black urban communities were nothing more than savage enclaves offering adverse consequences to anyone who chose to live there.

Without question the American dream advocates economic stability and individual accomplishments: having life-sustaining employment, living in a safe community with excellent schools, and accumulating wealth and prosperity. However, this dream is controlled by race-based policies that support exclusionary closure while advancing privileges, including privileges that ensure ownership of houses in the suburbs, excellent schools, generations of college graduates, and generational wealth, as well as privileges that eliminate competition from people of color to build social capital and thus remove disparities associated with health, education, and housing. The power to create hypersegregated schools that isolate children of color in academically low-performing schools increases their chances of dropping out of high school, and having skills associated with the future of work. The same power influences employment choices, wages, salaries, and wealth for students of color. All of these are closure strategies that widen the wealth gap between those with privileges and those without.

Racialized Perceptions

Racialized perceptions influence what individuals construe as "good" neighborhoods and schools. Racialized perceptions of what is "good" influence resegregation, which is controlled by affluent white home buyers whose status determines what is "good" housing and school choices (Wells, 2018). The reputation of schools is socially constructed with social stratification and based on racial biases. School reputations are not entirely objective and vary in terms of the social status of students enrolled. This process creates a strong correlation between wealthy individuals and wealthy school districts where the status of the neighborhood and schools relies on social status (Caplow & Finsterbusch, 1964). Individuals with the most money and valued cultural capital are linked to more school resources, higher academic outcomes, and higher property values. Thus, communities composed of mostly low-income Blacks and Hispanics are rarely, if ever, considered to be highly reputable or "desirable communities" (Wells, 2018). Reputations of neighborhoods and school districts are socially constructed, and the reputations exist within residents' imaginations (Griswold, 1992). Through their symbolic meaning of their resources as well as the people who live in their community, individuals create a desired reputation. This is particularly true for whites who view changing racial demographics in suburban communities negatively when there are racial and ethnic changes. This bias is correlated with the perceived status of new students entering public schools, especially students of color. This further supports the argument that whites devalue diverse neighborhoods and schools even if there are no tangible differences between where their live and other neighborhoods with larger populations (Wells et al., 2014). Overall, affluent school districts and communities create imaginary worlds that symbolically support their status and white privilege. Any changes in their imaginary world by elements of color are disruptive.

School choice, often based on reputation and community status, is especially influenced by race and education status of parents. According to Sikkink and Emerson (2008), educated whites see the racial composition of schools as a factor in school choice. When the percentage of Blacks living in a residential area increases, whites are far more likely to seek alternative schools with higher percentages of white students. While this trend is amplified by educated whites, this pattern is not the case for educated Blacks. The higher the educational attainment level of whites, the greater the negative sensitivity toward Blacks in public schools. Ultimately, decreasing the number of white students in some school district, increases resegregation for schools left with majority populations of Black and Hispanic students. School resources and financial support increasingly flow to prominent white school districts and, as a result, school inequalities increase when children of color and their families are isolated and resegregated from wealth.

Affluent whites and highly educated parents correlate school quality with reputations of schools, which are constructed through their social groups. The influence of their social network on community status and school choice is extraordinarily strong when making decisions as to where they will live and schools their children will attend (Wells, 2015). Saporito & Lareau (1998) found that white parents avoid schools with large Black student populations. Even when schools are in affluent neighborhoods, whites link the low social status of Blacks in society to low-performing schools. This line of thought supports research indicating that most affluent white parents do not fully embrace diversity in school choice. They prefer white school districts even when they know the benefits of diversity (Laciren-Paquet & Brantley, 2012).

People of color are asked to identify their race in American society. However, if you are white, no one will ask you to identify your race; it is assumed. Whiteness is like psychological money in the bank that is cashed every day by whites (Rothenberg, 2008). In the twenty-first century, whites are not focused on the cost of racism, symbolic racism, silent racism, subtle racism or new racism. Whites are more likely to focus on benefits that radiate, consciously or unconsciously, toward white privileges in education and housing choices that are supported by closure strategies. Fueled by the wealth gap between whites and non-whites, school resegregation becomes a more permanent design in society that constructs both social, economic, and racial boundaries, which place people of color, especially Blacks and Hispanics, permanently in resegregated communities and school districts that represent all the elements associated with inequality. Historically, segregation structured the schooling process year after year for students of color. When their families found diverse communities and excellent public schools, both the communities and schools slowly deconstructed by decreases in social services and school district financial support. If privilege allows some individuals to socially construct racialized perceptions, avoid encounters with diversity, and promote biases about race and school quality, then resegregation and socioeconomic stratification destroy school choice for people of color. Thus, resegregation operates as a process by which privilege and wealth permanently secure inequality in education for students of color.

Racialized barriers forever define educational attainment disproportionately for Black and Hispanic students. Without a strong educational foundation and work-related skills, you cannot emerge into adulthood with social, economic, cultural, and civic life as defined by our nation (Rudd, 2019). Further, racial isolation diminishes aspirations to achieve by building incalculable amounts of disparity, inequality, and segregation. By creating structural barriers to opportunity with segregated low-opportunity communities, inadequate health care, inadequate affordable housing, high unemployment and underemployment, underfunded schools, and distorted conceptualizations of who has access to higher education, collectively and independently structural racism removes life support for students of color (Rudd, 2019).

In the twenty-first century there are powerful forces building racialized barriers that influence educational outcomes for Black and Hispanic students despite their being aware of the fact that education is an opening to opportunity, and failure in education determines an individual's access to housing, health care, civic engagement, employment, and the ability to build wealth within one's lifetime (Rudd, 2019). Add the influences of racial bias, and students of color encounter diminished teacher expectations, cultural deficit thinking, and a buildup of toxic stress, which presents a significant negative impact on learning. In the United States, the mis-education of the emerging majority population in public schools, students of color, destroys a wealth of potential knowledge while firmly indicating how racism is woven into the fabric of our nation, relentless, and designed uphold white privilege.

Inequalities and College Admissions

Without question privilege can guarantee entrance to elite schools where wealth and privilege are far more likely to secure acceptance. The process ranges from politically connected applicants to gifts given to universities for as much as $3 million before an applicant even applies. Elite schools consider special categories such as legacy, family donations, children of faculty, and athletes as categories for admission.

The 2019 college admissions scandal further demonstrates the wealth gap in the United States and how wealthy white families have the resources to buy college acceptance. Low-income families, on the other hand, are simply resegregated and stranded in schools and neighborhoods that deny opportunities and control their life trajectory in society. This process is further exacerbated by property taxes that fund public schools in the United States. Naturally, low-income resegregated communities have extraordinarily little to contribute toward financing public education whereas powerful individuals with millions of dollars have the option to buy college acceptance indirectly, socially, and outright for their children.

Recent research indicates that access to colleges is influenced by the income level of a student's parents. Parents who are in the top 1 percent of income are 77 times more likely to send their children to an Ivy League college than a parent at the bottom income quintile. And just as interesting, the fraction of students from low-income families attending elite private colleges between 2000 and 2011 did not change but did fall sufficiently at colleges with the highest rates of bottom-to-top quintile mobility (Chetty et al., 2017).

Standardized Test Scores

When standardized test scores are posted online, schools are ranked and status hierarchies are created, which in turn provide prestige to schools with the highest scores and the students that attend those schools (Wells, 2018). Without access to the most prestigious schools, a systematic exclusion begins especially for students of color who are less likely to attend prestigious schools, have lower standardized test scores, and are permanently associated with low academic performance that determines their access to employment.

In 1917 psychologists used tests to measure the intelligence of Army recruits, and by 1923, Carl Brigham, one of the men who developed intelligence tests, published a study that implied that the decline of America's intelligence was rapidly associated with the presence of the Negro. Brigham believed that without public response to this knowledge, the decline would continue. After blaming Negroes for the demise of America's intelligence, there were concerns about immigrates arriving in America and attending public schools. However, these concerns did not prompt the removal of test bias.

According to Knoeset & Au (2017), the intrinsic components of standardized testing fuse with systems of school choice and function as mechanisms that use racial coding that supports segregation and inequalities in public schools. The segregation of children by race and class in public schools with the use standardized testing is deeply problematic. Understand that the purpose of education is not directed toward promoting a democratic society but more recently a focus on jobs and the economy (Apple, 2006). With education policies focused on jobs and the economy, there is less

need for integration in schools and, in 2019, schools in the United States mirror the 1950s in terms of segregation (Orfield, 2009).

According to the National Assessment of Educational Progress (NAEP), achievement gaps determine which students, grouped by various variables, outperform another group and if the difference in average scores for distinct groups are statistically significant. In reality, standardized testing is a tool based in racialized policies and reinforces white privilege. The use of standardized tests provides data that impacts schools, administrators, teachers, and students. The use of data from standardized tests, influences policies that formulate around education initiatives from charter schools, student growth, teacher evaluations, school closings, and Common Core standards (Au, 2007, 2009). Both data and policies support institutional racism, privilege, and disproportionately indicate that students of color are achieving below whites in a variety of subjects. For students of color, low achievement levels are linked to their families, cultures, teachers, and schools. However, seldom are these elements viewed as tools that enforce structural racism and social inequalities. Standardized testing occurs in grades K-12 and strongly correlates with structural racism and educational inequality in the form of collecting data and developing policies that are used to dismantle the education journey for students of color.

The No Child Left Behind (NCLB) federal law (2002) was an update of the Elementary and Secondary Education Act (1965) and designed to close the achievement gaps in race and socioeconomic background of students in public schools. NCLB was implemented after the 2001 recession and the longest lasting recession, the Great Recession (2007-2009). According to Leachman & Mai (2014), states began cutting school funding because of the Great Recession and, by 2014, 31 states provided less funding per student than in 2008. This meant over 350,000 teachers, school employees, and staff of education support services lost their jobs.

An analysis by the Education Law Center and Rutgers University of the report titled Is School Funding Fair? A National Report Card (2019), states that while school funding levels vary dramatically along school district lines and based on local property taxes, wealthy children receive double the funding rate of poor and low-income students.

Even in the most affluent state school systems, less funding is provided to high-poverty school districts even though research supports the concept that more money for resources in low-performing school districts increases achievement levels. Yet, the very districts that require more resources to achieve and experience a quality education receive less and less money each year. In 2015, Congress passed Every Student Succeeds Act to replace NCLB and scaled back the federal role in K-12 education. So, compounded by the removal of school resources, district financial support (two major connections to poverty and resegregation), and the historical and contemporary use of achievement data to advance white privilege, students of color are forever embedded in the apartheid nature of educational inequality.

Deficit Thinking

The term deficit thinking implies that children of color and low-income students of color are not successful in achieving an education, and their parents dismantle academic success resulting from internal defects such as limited educability and inadequate family support (Valencia, 1997). The theory incorporates the genetic pathology model, the culture of poverty model, and the "at-risk" model to imply that students of color, poor students, and their families are responsible for school failure.

Using deficit thinking, students of color and their families cause their own failure socially, economically, and academically. Like the term "race," the social construct of deficit thinking comes complete with its own language to imply that poor students are culturally disadvantaged and socialized toward apathy and underachievement. Systemic factors are not accounted for in the deficit thinking model, especially segregation, inequalities in school financing, and curriculum differentiation. Neither are structural inequalities, which include racist policies that purposely exclude students of color and poor students from equal educational and overall optimal learning opportunities (Valencia, 1997).

Deficit thinking enforces negative, stereotypical, and prejudicial beliefs about students of color so much that educators interpret differences as elements associated with dysfunctions, disadvantages, and overall individual deficits. By contrast, teachers who embrace student differences as strengths are more likely to create culturally relevant curricula that is student-centered, eliminates barriers to learning, and assists students with reaching their potential (Ford, 2015).

Deficit thinking represents another tool in structural racism to dismantle educational opportunities for children of color and children who live in poverty. Combine deficit thinking with standardized testing, as structural tools, and students of color outcomes are embedded in racialized structures, which lead to racialized academic achievement outcomes (Valencia, 1997).

SAT Testing

Historically, with no design toward cultural differences, intelligence tests placed the performance of Black students at the end of the scale. Today, standardized tests consistently direct academic experiences of Black and Hispanic students from early childhood to college admissions. According to Fair Test (2019), on average, students of color score lower on college admission tests and Black males are disproportionally placed in special education based on test results. The use of standardized tests perpetuates racial inequality and has the power to influence the emotional and psychological state of the test taker.

SAT scores have an adverse impact on college admissions for students of color and there are marginal indications that the scores predict how applicants perform in college. Race and SAT scores are imperfect indicators of a student's success in higher education. However, racial stratification with standardized testing remains entrenched in higher education. In addition, the history of the SAT reflects bias in favor of white students as indicated by research completed by the Harvard Education Review in 2003 and 2010. The research states that in the SAT English section, the test was biased in favor of cultural norms for white students. Until 2016, obscure vocabulary words also favored students with access to expensive tutors and prep courses.

The 2019 scandalous manipulation of SAT scores included deception, fraud, bribing college officials, fake test scores, fake credentials, fake photographs, and using medical documents that indicated a student had a learning disability and thus was granted additional time to complete the exam. White parents paid between $200,000 and $6.5 million to William Rick Singer, the mastermind behind the manipulation scheme (Chappell & Kennedy, 2019). The amount of money parents paid indicates they can afford any and every privilege their children need for academic success. Instead, the parents benefited from someone taking the SAT test or a proctor changing the answers for their children. Parents paid for acceptance to what they perceived as prestigious colleges and universities admission letters. Without remorse, parents actively participated in a corrupt and illegal admissions system designed to benefit wealthy parents. The parents were charged with accepting bribes and conspiracy to commit mail fraud and Singer pleaded guilty to federal crimes, ranging from conspiracy to commit racketeering and money laundering (Chappell & Kennedy 2019).

The nature of structural racism is such that it participates in institutional practices that create policies to advance the privilege of whiteness and dismantles social, economic, and political opportunities for people of color. These policies and forces determine who receives an education and how much education is required to maintain their place (class) in the economy and how their labor benefits the economy. Further, the nature of racialized policies determines when and if you need to attend school or if your labor is far more essential than an opportunity to learn how to read and write. The same policies determine where people of color can and cannot obtain employment and the monetary level of their wages. When historically and culturally a society supports structural racism then racial inequalities exist in all systems by predetermining specific roles for people of color in society—roles that determine where individuals live, go to school, and how society formulates a relationship between their existence beside privilege.

A racialized society devalues elements associated with people of color such as communities where they live and schools in their communities. By using racialized perceptions, people of color are isolated in resegregated neighborhoods and schools without apologies. Persons of color are more likely to live in poverty, be imprisoned, drop out of high school, be unemployed, and experience poor health outcomes. Whereas the historical accumulation of white privilege promotes quality education, better jobs, higher wages, homeownership, and generational wealth.

Institutional racism uses a variety of tools to maintain privilege, including biased standardized test scores, which exclude students of color from equal opportunities in education. By emphasizing achievement gaps between white students and students of color, larger proportions of academic resources and school finances are allocated for wealthy white communities while students of color attend dilapidated schools with fewer and fewer elements that support equality in education. In the end, institutional racism and racialized perceptions advance more than achievement gaps. Collectively, they advance opportunity gaps between white students and students of color.

In the twenty-first century we can no longer depend on the presence of white students in public schools to achieve desegregation, racial balance, and some euphoric form of diversity. For many urban and suburban communities, balanced racial desegregation is a concept from the past—a concept further hindered by the deceasing number of white students and the increasing number of Black and Hispanic students attending public schools.

The United States has a historical practice of implementing extensive systemic racist policies that purposely countered desegregation, and one of the major results of these policies is resegregation of public schools. Since the late 1980s, decades of progress have succumbed to the removal of desegregation plans as school district decisions to return to neighborhood- based schools created racial imbalance and isolation (Orfield et al., 2002; Clotfelter, Vigdor, & Ladd, 2006). In addition, school choice data indicate that white families choose magnet, charter, and a variety of other school choices that exacerbate racial isolation and imbalance (Orfield et al., 2002).

A third factor is the long history of racial and ethnic segregation in housing patterns, which determines public school enrollment. More than any other factor, housing segregation between Blacks and whites is difficult to change even though the nation is

growing more diverse. Distinctions appear in urban and suburban communities along racial lines as racialized perceptions are perpetuated by segregation.

At the same time, starting with the 1990s, Black segregated communities divided along socioeconomic lines emerged, especially affluent Black suburban enclaves. Black families wanted better schools for their children, but the establishment of affluent Black suburban enclaves did not lead to better public schools for Black students.

7 RESEGREGATION IN PRINCE GEORGE'S COUNTY MARYLAND

From Segregation to Desegregation

Prince George's County is an excellent example of states and counties resisting the *Brown* decision with an extensive legal history related to dismantling segregated schools. Ironically, after resisting desegregation, implementing forced busing, and later creating a plan to phase out government-mandated busing, in 2020, students attend apartheid schools. Apartheid schools imply that students of color (Black and Hispanic) constitute 90-100 percent of the student population in a school district. Nationwide, 80 percent of Hispanic students and 74 percent of Black students attend schools where students of color represent 50-100 percent of the student population (Civil Rights Project Report, 2018).

Prince George's County Maryland is a prime example of the Black middle- class moving to suburbia, escaping urban violence, and seeking opportunities for their children to attend exceptional public schools where they can receive a quality education. Often considered a wealthy Black community, the county borders Washington, DC, and was part of the suburbanization movement that offered Blacks an opportunity to remove economic and geographical segregation and purchase stately homes in affordable, attractive, and safe neighborhoods.

Until 1954, Prince George's County maintained a dual school system that was segregated by state law. By the end of the school year 1953-54, the county had 95 elementary and secondary schools, and Blacks attended 24 segregated schools (Thornton & Gooden, 1997). From school years 1955-56 to 1964-65, the county adopted a freedom of choice plan where each student was assigned a school to attend under the dual-school system. The one exception, students could choose to attend a school of choice, provided their parents requested a transfer. The school board did not publicize the process, however, made the process difficult, and required students to submit transfer papers (Valien, 1955). Thus, most Black students continued their education in segregated schools. In 1964, Prince George's County revised its policy by implementing attendance zones based on the concept of neighborhood schools. The county's plan established school attendance areas for every school without regard to race, color, religion, or national origin. In addition, the county established attendance areas without gerrymandering or other unnatural boundaries. However, a study by the U.S. Commission on Civil Rights (1965-66) concluded that the school board used existing segregation in housing to minimize desegregation and cover-up conscious or unconscious racist tendencies.

By 1971, a group of Black parents in Prince George's County sued for noncompliance with the 1964 Civil Rights Acts. Judge Frank Kaufman stated that the school system, illegally segregated, must establish a busing plan to achieve desegregation by January 1973. The decision was based on the *Swann v. Charlotte-Mecklenburg Board of Education* case in which the Supreme Court unanimously upheld busing programs that advanced racial integration of public schools in 1971.

After a lengthy legal history to desegregate public schools in the county, in 1998, U.S. District Judge Peter J. Messitte approved a 6-year plan to phase out the 26-year-old U.S. government-mandated busing effort to desegregate public schools in Prince George's County. In 1999, students began attending their neighborhood schools. The county attendance boundaries were revised, new schools were built, and parents were provided options of allowing their students to remain at their current school. The history of forced desegregation ended.

However, the plan to remove forced busing, after considered by both residents and members of the school board, did include elements of classism. Black children and their families who were living in poverty and working-class communities expressed a desire to rescind the busing order. Simultaneously, middle-class Blacks did not want "ghetto" kids in their neighborhood schools, nor did they want large concentrations of poor and low-income children in a single school building (Holmes & De Witt, 1996).

Dr. Alvin Thornton, a member of the school board in 1996, saw a far broader perspective. Dr. Thornton noticed that practically half the students in Prince George's County Public Schools were receiving free and reduced lunch, 40 percent of the student population was living in poverty, the overall achievement gap between upper and lower-income children was enormous and persistent, and instructional resources were maldistributed. Dr. Thornton concluded that, without question, these issues were problematic and that some middle-class Blacks embraced the same prejudices as their white counterparts (Holmes & De Witt, 1996). Currently (2020), Dr. Thornton is once again the chairman of the Prince George's County School Board.

White Flight and Desegregation

White flight began as a racist reaction to desegregation in the 1950s. This reaction prevented Black students from attending the same schools as white students in urban communities while establishing and achieving higher social status for whites who moved to suburban communities. Banks, realtors, and redlining supported a process that hindered Black families desiring to buy homes in suburban communities. Finally, when middle-class Blacks moved out of urban communities into suburban communities, whites continued to move farther away once communities were 40 percent or more Black.

Demographic changes in Prince George's County define and explain how this predominantly white county in 1954 grew into one of the most self- segregated residential and school regions in the United States today. According to United States Census Data (2015), the county's population was 88 percent white in 1950 and 91 percent white in 1960. Blacks represented 12 percent of the county's population in 1950, and the population of Blacks decreased to 9 percent in 1960 as Blacks moved to Washington, DC, with the anticipation of obtaining low-skilled federal jobs.

By 1980, once again, the county's demographics changed, and from this point forward, the white population decreased, and the Black population increased. With the suburbanization movement in 1990, housing options for middle-class Blacks expanded. For over 27 years, Blacks moved to Prince George's County in massive numbers, and massive numbers of whites moved out of the county. By 2019, Blacks and Hispanics comprised a majority population at 93 percent (U.S. Census, 2019c).

As Prince George's County grew into a resegregated community, surrounding counties in the metropolitan area became increasingly diverse. According to the Brookings Institution (2007), between 1993 and 2004, approximately 60 percent of new residents moving to the county were Black. Despite the opportunity for Black middle-class families to participate in the suburbanization process, the income level of Blacks moving to the county was lower than the income level of whites moving out of the county.

Overall, the changing demographics of Prince George's County reflected a pathway to middle-class housing and communities for Blacks. A large numbers of working-class

Black families were able to find affordable housing, and low-income families, forced out of the nation's capital, saw Prince George's County as a housing alternative.

Ironically, in 2020, Black and Hispanic families living in suburban areas like Prince George's County, especially communities next to metropolitan cities, experience increases in housing resegregation, social isolation, and elevated levels of poverty. Since 1999, the concentration of poverty in Prince George's County has increased.

Racism, Housing Policies, and Segregation

Prince George's County offered a significant opportunity to Black middle- class families, especially home ownership. However, this opportunity came with the influence of structural racism. After decades, in 2020, Prince George's County is a resegregated community that experiences increasing levels of poverty, missing social and public services, declining student academic performance, predator loans, and housing foreclosures. Still, questions remain whether this affluent Black enclave faces a painful reality, given that they cannot control racialized external factors.

Race-based policies established by the Federal Housing Authority (FHA), for so many years and before the suburbanization movement, purposely excluded Black Americans from living in suburban communities. Suburban communities offered outstanding school districts and opportunities to build economic wealth through increases in property values. However, the FHA's Underwriting Manual (1938) clearly stated that neighborhood stability depended on individuals of the same social and racial classes; otherwise, properties would experience instability, and housing values would decrease. This statement supported segregated neighborhoods by race and class, and decreased the probability of Black homeownership and their accumulation of property wealth.

Discrimination in housing, banned by the 1968 Fair Housing Act, initially received limited enforcement by the federal government. In 1974, the Equal Credit Opportunity Act outlawed race-based discrimination in mortgage lending, and in 1977 the Community Reinvestment Act banned redlining, an institutional practice of refusing mortgages to purchase homes in Black or racially mixed neighborhoods (Jackson, 1986). Even with changes in housing laws, the long historical systematic segregation that Blacks experienced in the housing market contributed to other economic inequalities as well — social and economic segregation, prejudice, and discriminatory beliefs that are difficult to reverse. As a result, Black middle-class neighborhoods are characterized by poverty, higher crime, inferior quality public schools, and fewer services compared to white middle-class neighborhoods (Pattillo-McCoy, 1998).

As much as affluent Blacks try, racialized perceptions prevent them from replicating exclusive white suburbs with high-quality schools, low property taxes, and overall desired amenities. Between 1994 and 1998, for example, Prince George's County witnessed a substantial decline in property values, especially as the northern parts of the county attracted low- and moderate-income individuals from Washington, DC. At the same time, the county's social distress indicators increased, and both child poverty and crime increased.

In some cases, affluent Blacks in Prince George's County moved to neighboring Charles County, Maryland to seek a better quality of suburban life and education equality for their children (Fletcher, 1998). However, between 2000 and 2010, the white population in Charles County, Maryland declined by 11 percent, the Black population increased by 91 percent, and the Hispanic population increased by 130 percent. In 2019, 43 percent of whites, 43 percent of Blacks, and 5 percent of Hispanics lived in the county. Blacks and Hispanics represent 48 percent of the population and whites are gradually moving out of the county (Population of Charles County Maryland, 2019). These statistics further indicate a sign of white flight when suburban communities become more than 40 percent people of color. At the same time, they also increase the likelihood that the quality of public education may decrease, property values may decrease, school funding may decrease, and the county will experience an increase in poverty.

Throughout the United States, evidence indicates that affluent Black suburban communities experience racialization, poverty, higher crime rates, fewer public services, and resegregated schools with low standardized test scores. Ultimately, only predominantly white suburbs illustrate the ideal suburban community with all the amenities, and less social service burdens (Cashin, 2005). One reaction to the disappointment and inability to create a utopic community is an air of classism by affluent Blacks. For example, when Black urban basketball players used public courts in an affluent Prince George's County community, neighbors hired a private security company to filter out non-residents. There is a certain irony in Blacks hiring Blacks to protect Blacks from Blacks.

While the gratifying social status of moving to an affluent Black suburb led to political power, this type of separatist position comes with a steep cost in Prince George's County—a cost influenced by systemic forces that economically dismantle even affluent Blacks (Cashin, 2001). After a long history of housing and public school segregation, affluent Blacks in Prince George's County increasingly live in resegregated communities as whites move out, property values decrease, and education equality is not achieved in public schools. This is a frustration that has been created by structural racism, which dismantles education equality, social achievement, and academic achievement for Black families in suburban communities.

The Box Theory in Predominantly Black Enclaves

Fairwood, a subdivision in Prince George's County with over 1,800 sprawling homes, is considered the wealthiest neighborhood in Prince George's County. Built on a former slave plantation, the community was part of the housing boom in 2006 and 2007. Construction of Fairwood started in 2001, the first homes were ready by 2003, and by 2006 the community expanded. The promise that Prince George's County would build a new elementary school for the community lured Fairwood homeowners, and parents believed that wealthy communities would be more likely to produce high academic performing students. In 2011 the community organized a task force to persuade the school board, but as of 2020, there are no plans to build a new elementary school for the community.

Sadly, half the home loans foreclosed, and in some parts of the subdivision, 20 of the 34 homes on one block fell into foreclosure. Between 2006 and 2008, 173 homes purchased in Fairwood foreclosed, and 43 homeowners financed their homes for 100 percent of the cost (Kelly et al., 2015). The community had the second-highest foreclosure rate in Prince George's County. The previous imagined community with million-dollar homes, now sell for a fraction of the original cost in 2019. In some cases, over $300,000 less than the original asking price (Kelly et al., 2015).

While the mortgage crisis disproportionately impacted Blacks nationwide, residents of Prince George's County lost more wealth than families in neighboring majority-white suburban communities, and the county became the center for mortgage failure in Maryland. Overall, Prince George's County homeowners experienced extensive and abusive predation targeted toward Blacks and Hispanics.

Residents of Prince George's County and other Black suburban enclaves believe that segregated Black suburbs can experience the suburban ideal of high-quality schools, amenities, low taxes, and services. Author Pattillo- McCoy (2013) implies that this expectation is dubious, given that Black suburbs cannot counteract the negative externalities that generate from decisions made by public and private sectors outside of their borders. In general, Black middle-class neighborhoods are characterized by poverty, higher crime, inferior quality public schools, and fewer services compared to white middle-class neighborhoods (Pattillo-McCoy, 2013). Thus, the nature of structural racism is such that it provides consistent opportunities to widen the wealth gap between white families and families of color. These gaps then transfer from one generation to the next by removing education equality, life-sustaining employment, and overall well-being, especially for students in public schools.

Racial isolation harms middle-class Blacks and their school-age children as predominantly Black schools attract elevated levels of students living in low-income families and poverty. The complexities of social class confront the Black middle-class who cannot disconnect from Blacks who are poor and are likely to be their relatives as well. The Black middle-class sits at the doorstep of privilege but cannot disconnect from the need for continued affirmative action, access to higher education, and the abatement of residential segregation (Pattillo-McCoy, 2013).

Over the past three decades, the most affluent families added net worth, but the bottom 90 percent of families dipped into negative wealth where their debts exceed their assets. The median white family has 41 times more wealth than the median Black family and 22 times more wealth than the median Latino family (Forbes, 2019). This is a divide that determines which families are more likely to encounter educational inequalities in public schools.

As the wealth gap between whites and people of color increases, the more intense the disparities become for students of color in resegregated schools and communities that isolate them. Two of the major disparities are social achievement and academic achievement. The higher the socioeconomic level of families, the more isolated they are from people of color, and the more likely they are to live in communities that receive an abundance of school financing, resources, and opportunities for students to engage with the best teachers in the school district. The collective nature of structural racism is such that it determines that white and Asian students have less exposure to Blacks and Hispanic students, and they cultivate into the most advantaged groups in terms of educational outcomes. Thus, the wealth gap includes an increase in the social achievement gap and the academic achievement gap for students of color.

The nature of Black segregated suburban enclaves creates a situation similar to living in a box—a box in which individuals live, work, shop, and attend schools that are designed by structural racism. This box permanently and consistently creates disparities and inequalities regardless of overall achievements by the Black middle-class—a box that destabilizes the community, undermines their access to opportunity, and creates structural barriers to housing, healthcare, employment, and education.

Resegregation and Students of Color

Blacks in Prince George's County fought from 1954 to 1973 to desegregate public schools before students began attending their neighborhood schools in 1999. However,

Black parents did not anticipate white flight so much that in 2019, students of color are 91 percent of the public school population and attend resegregated schools. With a total white student population of almost 5,300 students in 2019, there is no chance of the county's public schools achieving racially balanced integration.

Prince George's County Public Schools (PGCPS), one of the largest school districts in the United States, the second-largest district in the state of Maryland, enrolled 132,322 students in 2018 (Maryland State Department of Education, 2019). A breakdown of the district's student population by race in 2018 indicates that Black students are the majority population at 58 percent, followed by Hispanic students at 33 percent, white students at 4 percent, and Asian students at 3 percent. Together Blacks and Hispanic students represented 91 percent of the county's student population in 2018 (Maryland State Department of Education, 2019).

Nevertheless, why should the racial composition of public schools determine academic outcomes, especially for students of color? Why does self- segregation in Black communities and resegregation of public schools advance inequalities for children of color who are the majority population? Is the dismantling of public school education in Prince George's County consciously driven by elements of structural racism and the economic impact of the racial wealth gap? Last, what is the future of work for students of color who attend resegregated schools?

In 2020, PGCPS are still attempting to establish successful educational reforms and improve academic achievement gaps for all students, regardless of their socioeconomic level. Most of the funding for the school districts comes from property taxes, and Prince George's County has the highest property taxes compared to surrounding jurisdictions in the Washington, DC , metropolitan area (Department of Assessment and Taxation, 2019).

Prince George's County Public Schools (PGCPS) per-pupil revenues for students in 2018 was $16,250. This revenue combines local, state, and federal funding. PGCPS ranks 8th in terms of school districts receiving the highest percentage of state funding (59 percent) and 17th in terms of percentage allocated by local funding (36.4 percent), based on 23 counties and Baltimore City Public Schools (Overview of Maryland, 2018).

In 2019, the Prince George's County Council passed a $4.1 billion dollar budget that includes $2.5 billion dollars for public schools, an increase of $72.3 million dollar over the fiscal year 2018 budget. Interestingly, this increase represents an increase of $133 million since the fiscal year 2015 (McNamara, 2019). Conversely, with substantial funding for students in the public schools, the county ranks next to last for student overall academic performance in the state, and county students have not demonstrated consistent academic achievement, especially in English language arts (ELA) and mathematics.

Within Prince George's County Public Schools, the student population consists of an extremely high concentration of low-income students and students living in poverty, as well as a majority of the student enrollment (60 percent) who qualify for the Free and Reduced-Price Meals (FARM) program. These facts are compelling, given that data are indicating that students of color and family income impacts educational success and outcomes. Black students living in resegregated suburbs, the idea of high-quality schools and low taxes are entwining with systemic disadvantages that slowly dismantle equality in education and well-being. As a result, Prince George's County is not a wealthy majority-Black jurisdiction in the United States, given that within the surrounding metropolitan area, the county has the lowest property values, the lowest median household income, and the lowest overall student academic outcomes.

America is a country that implemented segregated public policies and racist institutional practices, exercised cultural marginalization, and perpetuated racial inequity while allowing privileges for whites and disadvantages for people of color, especially Blacks. Historically, Prince George's County economic development indicates a county rooted in all the elements of structural racism. Structural racism impacts the social, economic, and political systems within a community, and the county's journey from a segregated landscape to a resegregated landscape is evident. Blacks have obtained political power, suburban housing, and for a brief time, desegregated schools. Nevertheless, can a segregated majority Black suburban enclave and its residents design a community that offers education equality to all students, especially if public school success aligns with moving all citizens out of poverty and into economic prosperity?

Gaps in social and academic achievement require both schools and communities to develop drastic reforms. In Prince George's County, the future of work for Black and Hispanic children relies on the economic intersectionality of multiple factors, (i.e., race and education), which are associated with economic disadvantage (Mason, 2019). If disparities in educational attainment exist, income disparities will exist as well for the majority population in the county.

In 2030, Black employment will be disrupted by automation, digital technologies, and the persistent growth of a racial wealth gap between whites and people of color (Cook et al., 2019). Extreme polarization of wealth, racialized inequalities (economic and education), poverty, and resegregation are significant tools in structural racism that consume Prince George's County. Thus, will students of color attending public schools in Prince George's County be eliminated from the future of work in the United States?

Poverty and Public Education

According to Jonah Edelman (Taylor, 2019), poverty significantly impacts a child's academic achievement at an early age, challenges a student's cognitive and literacy ability, and places children living in poverty socioeconomically, and academically behind peers from higher-income families. Families living in resegregated communities and poverty struggle to provide food, clothing, shelter, and ideal child development environments as well. Children in these environments are at risk in their education journey, unlikely to complete their formal education, and more likely to repeat grades. Beyond education deficiencies in secondary education, poverty hinders access to financial resources and, thus, the ability to obtain post-secondary education or training.

The poverty rate in Prince George's County improved when middle-class Blacks migrated from Washington, DC. However, Prince George's County disproportionately attracted more low-income individuals than the surrounding communities (Dent, 1992). Recently, the influx of low-income and poverty-level families who cannot afford to live in Washington, DC, changed the county's poverty rate—again. In 2018, the county's overall poverty rate was nearly 9 percent and 11 percent for children under 18 years of age lived at the poverty level (U.S. Census, 2017c). Between 1980 and 1990, 54 county communities experienced an increase in child poverty, especially communities in the western part of the county (Orfield, 1999). Within 2018, 72 communities had double-digit poverty rates.

The Supplemental Nutrition Assistance Program (SNAP), formerly known as food stamps, is designed to provide nutrition options to low-income households. In 2016, nearly 91,000 individuals in Prince George's County received SNAP benefits (U.S. Census Bureau, 2017d). By 2017, nearly 11 percent of children ages 5-17, and their families lived in poverty (U.S. Census Bureau, 2017c).

Another measure of poverty includes the Free and Reduced Meals (FARMs) program, which offers a proxy measure for the percentage of students living in poverty. In Prince George's County, nearly 62 percent of students (76,375) enrolled in public schools in 2018 were eligible for FARM. The FARM program in 2019 represented 60 percent of the county's student enrollment or 77,325 students, a 1.2 percent increase from 2018 (Maryland Department of Legislative Services, Office of Policy Analysis, 2019).

Numerous factors contribute to families living in low-income and poverty environments, and indeed, minimum wages can assist in alleviating income inequality, especially for low-skilled wage workers. The current minimum wage (2020) in Prince George's County is $11.50 per hour. Employees age 18 and under and working less than 20 hours per week are exempt but must earn at least 85 percent of the state minimum wage, which is $11.00 per hour. Compared to surrounding communities, the minimum wage in Washington, DC, is $15 per hour for all workers regardless of the size of the business. The minimum wage in Montgomery County, Maryland is $14 per hour for employers with 51 or more employees, $13.25 per hour for employers with 50 or fewer employees, and, like Prince George's County, individuals under 18 years of age must receive 85 percent of the state minimum wage (Maryland Minimum Wage, 2019).

Both low wages and poverty harm the well-being of families, affecting their ability to survive, and raise children in healthy environments. Likewise, the nature of resegregated communities is such that it impacts median household income, property values, and resources in public schools (Maryland Poverty Rate County Comparison, 2019). School district revenue, based on property taxes, must adjust to declines in property values. Thus, school revenue can significantly impact students living in high-poverty communities in terms of academic achievement and outcomes, especially if these communities receive less school financial support than wealthier communities.

Any number of reasons can indicate a decline in students achieving proficiency from year to year; however, when the pattern occurs in high-poverty neighborhoods where students of color live in resegregated communities, the loss is exceptionally significant as students do not recover during their education journey.

Poverty influences education equality and creates an extraordinarily complex system of educational inequality. There are no immediate solutions to address the complex nature of poverty and inequality in education unless communities address both issues simultaneously. There are school districts that adamantly change the influence of poverty with economic empowerment for low-income families and provide students of color in resegregated communities with the best resources associated with academic success, especially the best teachers. Collectively, the changes occur by organizing around the same mission.

Racial Bias and Standardized Testing

The Maryland Comprehensive Assessment Program (MCAP) profiles each county in the state in terms of student progress toward academic proficiency, especially in terms of English language arts and mathematics. During the school year 2017-18, overall elementary, middle, and high schools in PGCPS did not meet the annual target in academic achievement (Maryland State Department of Education, 2019). For Black elementary students, 21 percent were proficient in math, and 30 percent were proficient in English language arts (ELA). For Hispanic elementary students, 17 percent were proficient in math and 21 percent were proficient in ELA. Whereas for white elementary students were 43 percent were proficient in math and 51 were percent proficient in ELA, Asian elementary students had the highest proficiency levels, 49 percent for math, and 54 percent for ELA.

Middle school and high school students presented the same pattern in scores where Asian students had the highest percentage of proficiency followed by whites, Blacks, and then Hispanic students (Maryland State Department of Education, 2018). The causes for poor student performance in Prince George's County Public Schools are not clearly understood, at least financially given that the county has a high per-pupil revenue.

Taken as a whole, public schools in the United States are among the most inequitable in terms of funding in the industrialized world. Inequalities impact teacher quality, limit school resources, and diminish curriculum choices, especially for students of color. The more severe the disparities that manifest in public education, the more compelling the influence on student academic outcomes, especially for low-income students. Without question, ideal school resources, choice curriculum, and teacher expertise can combine to ensure higher student achievement for low-income students by improving academic outcomes and graduation rates. Research indicates that increasing per-pupil spending by 21.7 percent for low-income children throughout all 12 school-age years eliminates the education attainment gap between low-income and non-poor students and increases the graduation rates by 20 percentage points for low-income children (Baker, 2018).

However, performance on standardized testing for students of color is complicated. Some scholars believe that performance differences between students of color and whites result from a person's genetic composition or cultural factors. But reality strongly indicates that the mere nature of standardized testing for over a century is affected by bias and racism. Nevertheless, students of color begin to encounter standardized testing in early childhood and continue through college admissions testing (Rosales, 2019). According to Lee & Orfield (2006), neither a significant rise in achievement nor closure of racial achievement gaps were realized even though the federal government provided over $400 million under the No Child Left Behind Act to end "soft racism of low expectations" and thus, close racial achievement gaps within eight years. The goal with the use of mandated yearly tests, which were required for elementary and middle school students from all racial and ethnic groups was to attain 100 percent proficiency in math and reading (science was added later) and to eliminate the achievement gap by ethnicity, race, language, and special education status. Only small gains in math were realized and overall, the government efforts were counterproductive.

This massive effort by the federal government did not address the impact of large- scale school resegregation nor the cost of double segregation by poverty and race (Frankenberg et al., 2019). Between the 1970s and 1980s, school integration efforts were overwhelmingly successful and students who attended integrated schools, especially schools that were well-funded, were more successful in life regardless of race (Johnson, 2019). But since 1988, segregation has prevailed, the wealth gap between whites and people of color has increased, and education inequalities are increasing for students of color as they attempt to enter the workforce.

Further, it is imperative to acknowledge that resegregation in communities and public school districts that children of color attend is designed by structural racism—a design that isolates individuals into low-income and high- poverty communities and contributes to low academic achievement. Thus, in Prince George's County, public schools fail to meet annual academic targets at all school levels because of resegregation, segregated housing patterns, epidemic poverty levels, and race-based systematic inequalities. The very nature of these inequalities removes students of color from the future of work in the economy which requires relationship skills and soft skills that include inherent social cues, communication abilities, and interactions with others outside one's own ethnicity.

The Future of Work

The most daunting challenges for Prince George's County Public Schools are beyond raising standardized test scores given that technological innovations, robots, and computers are changing America's workplace. If students of color—the majority student population in the county's public schools—are not job-ready, employable, and have an acquisition of skills when they leave the schoolhouse, the future of work will not exist for students who attend public schools in Prince George's County (White, 2019).

As recent high school graduates' journey toward post-secondary education and job training, they face a workplace that requires the use of technology and automation—a workplace that assumes workers can use technology without spending work-related hours being trained. Employers expect employees to be active problem-solvers and embrace the efficiencies associated with technology in the workplace.

If students of color leave secondary schools without skills for the digital and global economy, they are less likely to obtain those skills later in life, especially students who attend resegregated schools and live in low-income communities. This population may never find employment if they are lacking skills related to critical thinking, creativity, communication, analysis of data, managing data, software development, computer programming, digital security and privacy, business process, project management, digital design, communication of data, and collaboration (The New Foundational Skills of the Digital Economy, 2019). Skills that determine employment and the ability to transition from one job to another are essential. Member of the new workforce are likely to have 5-7 jobs during their lifetime.

The new workplace will not guarantee job security or retirement benefits, create pathways to new work opportunities, or offer employer-provided training. Employees, who do not invest their earned income in training or have financial constraints when trying to obtain additional job training, are likely to experience work-related barriers that may lead to unemployment or underemployment. Further, government agencies and policies are far less likely to provide any type of income assistance or solutions for job displacement (White, 2019).

Without personal resources to obtain post-secondary education and training, students of color are less likely to attend college, have access to online colleges, and participate in job training programs. Besides, policymakers and employers designing opportunities for tuition-assistance programs are likely to deny this opportunity for employees who require remediation. Current research indicates that 40-60 percent of first-year college students require remediation in both math and English, a detriment that increases their likelihood of dropping out of college.

According to McKinsey (2019), in the next 10 years, Blacks in America could lose 4.5 million jobs, 10 percent more jobs than the general population. Jobs that can be replaced by artificial intelligence, software, and robots are the same jobs that low-wage and low-skill workers are assigned. At the same time, Black males are over-represented in high-displacement jobs that include food services, retail workers, office support, and factory workers. Jobs lost to automation can only be mitigated by higher education, and Black males are underrepresented in this population, including graduate degrees. Overall, in the next 10 years, the employment outlook for Blacks, especially young workers between the ages of 18-35, and without a college degree, is disturbing.

Prince George's County represents one of the largest school districts in Maryland and the nation, with over 132,000 students the majority of whom are students of color. If this or any other school district, with majority students of color, fails to prepare students for life-sustaining employment and the future of work, student well-being is horrendously grim. If students of color do not receive a public education that links them to middle-class and in-demand jobs, they are placed in low-skilled jobs and inevitably forced into unemployment, underemployment, and the prison pipelines.

School districts can continue to invest in race-based standardized testing or invest in career-and-technical programs. Programs that are more responsive to changes in the job market, that support the entrance to a two- or four-year college, and provide opportunities for students of color to enter and stay in a global economy will also support positive school culture and alleviate the stressor of not having a future.

The following is a message from the homepage of Prince George's County Public Schools website (November 5, 2019).

Located just minutes away from Washington, D.C., Prince George's County offers easy access to the nation's political, cultural and entertainment center. The vibrant Washington corridor boasts historical sites and museums, top universities and colleges, and a high quality of living.

Prince George's County Public Schools (PGCPS), one of the nation's 25 largest school districts, has 208 schools and centers, more than 130,000 students and nearly 19,000 employees. The school system serves a diverse student population from urban, suburban and rural communities located in the Washington, DC suburbs. PGCPS is nationally recognized for innovative programs and initiatives that provide students with unique learning opportunities, including arts integration, environmental and financial literacy, and language immersion.

The Board of Education works to advance student achievement through community engagement, sound policy governance, accountability and fiscal responsibility. The school system's highest priority is to prepare students to meet the demands of college and careers.

8 RACE AND EDUCATION

Changing Demographics

Changing demographics in America are resulting in dramatic transformations in the fabric of our nation. These transformations have a radical affect on students of color and the delivery of public education. According to the National Center for Education Statistics 2016, Black and Hispanic children make up the majority population in public schools. Whereas white children who attend public schools, are increasingly isolated in majority-white school districts or charter schools that select their populations. Thus, it is not by chance that students of color attend resegregated public schools.

The United States has a consistent schooling history that promotes racialization, racism, and institutional conditions that do not support students of color. Even *Brown v. Board of Education of Topeka* did not and could not deconstruct the practice of racism and the will to continue white supremacy. Instead, in response to *Brown* and the Civil Rights Movement, the majority white population found opportunities to advance the creativity of new and more formidable tools to support racism in educational institutions throughout the United States. Institutional racism, like Alabama Governor George Wallace's speech in 1963, implies "segregation now, segregation tomorrow, segregation forever." Thus, in the twenty-first century, public education for students of color is laced with elements from a "new racism" (Bonilla-Silva, 2015) in order to maintain white privilege.

For students of color, institutional racism does not manifest in mysterious ways. Students of color are far more likely to experience blatant encounters in public schools that are serious and traumatizing. Their experiences include far more confrontations with being suspended, expelled, and criminalized. Even pre-school students of color are

111

far more likely to be suspended, especially Black students who represent nearly half of pre-school suspensions (U.S. Department of Education, 2017e). Children of color who attend public schools experience exclusion from gifted and talented programs but are far more likely to be placed disproportionately in special education classes. These elements are compounded by racially biased standardized testing, manipulated curriculums, and decreases in school finance and resources for majority Black and Hispanic schools. Further, this picture indicates that the resistance to *Brown* created institutional conditions, especially policies and laws within school districts, that permanently destroyed equality in education for students of color.

As the student population changes in public schools, so does the population of teachers who are likely to instruct children of color. Consistently, very few qualified teachers choose encounters with children of color except for Black Career Educators, who are the most significant and last generation of highly qualified teachers to engage with children of color. The largest generation of Black Career Educators, mostly baby boomers, is retiring (over 10,000 baby boomer teachers retire daily). Without this generation of teachers, children of color no longer have a buffer between the microaggressions associated with racism—microaggressions that invade and question their culture, persona, and personal style.

Most teachers in public schools (over 80 percent) are white and female. Without teachers of color, cultural differences between students and their teachers are difficult to bridge, especially for students who live in low-income communities and disadvantaged communities. This issue intensifies when school districts do not address cultural competence related to teachers.

Education Policies and Racism

Too often, education policies in the United States overlook the impact of America's changing demographics in public education. Nevertheless, public schools are the first reflection of trends in society. Trends that are impacting public education include growing racial segregation, poverty, immigration, gentrification, and inequality, and most of all, the growing wealth gap between whites and people of color.

Education policy in recent years has focused on increasing academic standards and public accountability to improve public education. However, these policies failed to improve educational opportunities for children of color, especially children living in low-income families, a majority population in public schools that represents 51percent of the public school students in the United States (Noguera, 2017).

Resegregation in public schools, more than any other trend associated with education inequality, is evident of the fact that students of color and their families live in segregated, low-income, and isolated communities. These environments do not offer social and economic opportunities for students of color to participate in a global society or for their families to obtain generational wealth. Besides, low-income students face more educational obstacles than students from wealthy families, and missed educational opportunities perpetuate the cycle of poverty. Just as slavery, Jim Crow laws, and segregation chastised students of color for low achievement levels, the current Apartheid nature of public education ensures that students of color in resegregated public schools will not have the academic and career skills to obtain employment in a society where the future of work will offer fewer and fewer jobs as the result of technology and automation.

New racist tools enforced by public education policies, such as the consideration of dismantling the federally supported Free and Reduced Meals Program (FARM), permanently ensure that children of color will no longer receive a free public school education. Many school districts in America are not equipped to address demographic and economic changes in their school population with adequate resources. With the use of new racist tools, school districts may require Black and Hispanic parents to pay for their children's secondary education provided, they meet the demands of educational policies, which are designed to remove them from public education and the workforce permanently. If the majority population in public schools, Black and Hispanic students, fails to meet the demands of new policies and standards, and their parents literally cannot afford to pay for their public school education, then institutional racism will only advance the Apartheid nature of the current public education system. Overall, from K-12, students of color are marginalized by racialized policies and practices that are designed to disrupt their academic potential and funnel them into the prison pipelines.

Teaching While Black

Brown v. The Board of Education of Topeka is, without a doubt, one of the most historical decisions related to public education in America. Legally, *Brown* attempted to remove America's version of Apartheid (Omi & Winant, 1986). However, the effectiveness of *Brown* has consistently receded to the point where Black Career Educators are steadily missing in public education, the halls of higher education, and children of color, especially Black and Hispanic students, attend resegregated public schools.

Even with a constitutional amendment, race and class still dominate and impact multiple aspects of higher education, public education, achievement gaps, bilingual education, school choice, school reform and performance, special education, and school discipline (Noguera, Pierce & Ahram, 2014). Also, in the mix is teaching while Black in America. Whether at the secondary or collegiate levels of education, Black educators are likely to experience racialized perceptions about their scholarship and the mental anguish associated with relational aggression, microaggressions, and macroaggressions in predominantly white teaching environments.

In 1997, I decided to leave secondary education for the collegiate level and taught for several years at predominantly white universities. My first job interview with white faculty members consisted of questions and a presentation. A panel of four white faculty members displayed a glossed-over look after my presentation, and only one member on the panel engaged in conversation related to the presentation. While all the faculty members were academically astute, collectively, the challenge of interviewing a Black female was apparent.

Sitting in front of an all-white senior faculty search committee confirmed the need for a person of color in the department. Ideally, the search committee should have invited a Black faculty member or a person of color from another department or individuals with similar scholarly and research backgrounds, to participate in the interview.

After the interview and lunch, a member of the committee called a taxi. However, the taxi driver was disappointed and majorly upset that I was not going to the airport, naturally a more expensive fare. Bold, free, and not in a mood for a debate, I exited the taxi and asked a gentleman sitting at a bus stop for directions to the train station. Fortunately for me, this was the bus stop that went directly to the train station.

Later that evening, the department chair called and informed me that the taxi driver said I jumped out of the cab, walked away, and was lost in an "urban city." She stated that search committee members drove to my rescue but could not locate my body. I am a city dweller, and I found the actions of the all suburban rescue team a little bazaar.

After the interview, the department chair requested additional support documents. In total, I submitted 47 additional pieces of paper beyond my curriculum vitae to solidify my qualifications and worthiness for the faculty position. All in all, there were four faculty members of color hired that summer. Three professors left because of stress related to racism.

If, for one moment in time, I believed, as a Black woman, that white Americans were smart simply because they are white, then I assure you that white college students totally dispelled that myth. White undergraduate and graduate students were agitated when taught by a Black woman with a Ph.D. from a research level-one university. For numerous students, I was the first person of color they encountered in pursuing an education. Even when exhibiting my best "Negro" behavior and parking any elements associated with the "Angry Black Woman Syndrome," racial microaggressions appear in my academic evaluations from students.

White students questioned the subject matter I taught, challenged my ability to instruct them, and were poised to ask numerous questions based on their perceptions of Black professors:

"How are you qualified to teach us?"
"I know you are Black by the size of your nose."

"Can you explain why my immigrant grandfather, who arrived from Italy with no money, fixed a broken lawnmower, and started a successful business is more successful than poor Blacks?"

"Why should we include urban schools in our student teaching experiences...we're not going to teach in an urban school."

"Why are the articles about Black people? "
"We're graduate students...why do we need to call you Dr. Alderman...can't we call you by your first name?"

Just imagine, undergraduate and graduate students determining if a Black faculty member is qualified to teach them and totally perplexed that I will not answer all their questions related to being Black in America. Their thoughts reveal a lack of cultural encounters outside of their ethnicity — a lack of experiences that leads to stereotyping individuals even when evidence dismisses their beliefs.

One evening after class, three white female students report that they were traumatized by an encounter with a Black faculty member. Their concerns were based on the professor assigning homework. A previous white faculty member who taught the course was known for creating an environment like a campfire chat. Thus, the mere thought of homework was genuinely alarming.

I tried to eat lunch with white colleagues at least once a week. During lunch, a senior male colleague claimed to be an expert about the establishment of Georgetown University in Washington, DC, my hometown. In conversation, he mentioned Patrick Francis Healy, and I immediately mentioned that Healy was the first Black president of the university. That colleague, if ever, was no longer an ally. He questioned the validity of my implication about Dr. Healy, implying that he and only he knew the full history of the university. During future encounters, he never acknowledged that I was right. Sometimes the presence of Black scholars is challenging to whiteness.

For five years, behind closed doors, faculty members and administrators allowed students to berate my teaching qualifications without any evidence to support their accusations. Concerned about an accusation, the department chair, a white female, entered my office one afternoon and insisted that I allow her to visit my undergraduate class. Given that her request was not based on an official evaluation, I had the option to deny her request. Relentless in her verbal pursuit, she leaned over my desk, raised her voice (my office door was open), and continued for 10 minutes to demand access to my class. I observed the red flow of blood under her skin, moving from the base of her neck into her face. At that point, I rose from my office chair and moved our conversation to the hallway. Her loud insistence was evident to other faculty members who lowered their heads and returned to their offices once we entered the hallway. I did not allow the department chair to visit my classroom, given that she was not supportive and had voiced resistance to being forced to hire a person of color. She preferred a white female candidate for the position. However, her selection was denied, given that the individual did not have a terminal degree (Ph.D.), and the department needed individuals of color for the upcoming accreditation process.

At the graduate level, the resistance to professors of color can be more challenging. For some white students, the mere existence of a Black professor is basely unacceptable under any circumstances. As a graduate student, I cannot imagine crying in class because I did not like the grade I received on an assignment. Having attended Howard University, professors would have suggested I exit the graduate program and escorted me to the university hospital. However, when you are white and female, there is a privilege— so, apparently your tears are worthy of attention.

Teaching at the collegiate level is where underlying racism creates multiple problems for both white students and administrators. Even when discussing materials related to people of color or race, white students implied that I was too Afrocentric. Thus, it is far easier to assume that Black faculty members are a problem than to address the underlying racism within an institution.

In every secondary school district, there are desirable schools where most educators would prefer to teach. One school had the highest percentage of white teachers and students in the district. When I arrived, I was one of two Black teachers and the only Black female in the department. While the Black male teacher has carved out an academic niche, it is evident that white teachers have priority as to what they desire to teach.

All schools have a culture that defines their atmosphere, policies, and expectations. Which teachers are in charge or think they are in charge, and which academic programs in the school are valued becomes evident. In this case, the most valued academic program is composed of white students and very few students of color. Teacher schedules are designed to accommodate the students in the program, grades are changed if necessary, and the parents resemble piranhas. They will eradicate any elements that do not align with their child's successful academic achievement.

Even individuals who are not educators, but white, exercise white privilege when engaging with Black educators. In one instance, a para-professional entered a classroom and demanded that the teacher should give less homework so that white female students could participate in after school activities. Demanding to see students' progress reports, but when denied (school policy), she seeks revenge. Failure to read the rule book on *How New Black Teachers Should Behave* can cause problems for Black educators in predominantly white schools.

At the secondary level, a Black teacher indicated that white parents scheduled parent/student conferences relentlessly even when their student's grade was an A. The intent, it seemed, was that if enough parents complained about a teacher of color, then surely the school's administration will dismiss the teacher as uniquely unqualified. This approach was supported by student evaluations that were subjective and based on teacher likability and how comfortable students felt in the teacher's class. Student evaluations that indicate a teacher is biased, "racist," and hates white students is a widespread student accusation toward Black teachers (Muhs, 2012).

In one school year, a Black teacher attended 52 parent conferences (approximately one-third of the school days). All but three conferences were with white parents who indicated that the Black teacher mistreated white students. One conference involved two parents who thought the teacher spoke hoarsely to their son. Their son opened the teacher's closet and started rummaging through her personal items. The parents demanded an apology for asking their son, "why are you in my closet?" The teacher refused to apologize. However, the parents continued to write harsh statements about the teacher (without evidence to support their statements) and forward them to the school board.

In an effort to remove another Black teacher, white parents wrote random letters to the school board about his performance as a teacher. In short, none of the letters provided evidence to support accusations. They were based on comments by students and their perceptions of events. Parents had not witnessed any events. Under pressure from parents and the possibility of not becoming the next principal of the school, the Black acting-principal violated the teacher evaluation procedures. The principal approached the teacher during one of his lessons and asked that he sign a form indicating he needed an additional evaluation to determine if he was an effective teacher. The teacher refused to sign the request.

The art of intimidating teachers is a widespread practice, but race accelerates the process. Yet another Black teacher was placed under the supervision of a subject supervisor who would conduct a teacher evaluation. A white male parent accused the Black teacher of being retaliatory toward his son, who was an excellent student. Later in the school year, the supervisor met with the student and determined that the student genuinely enjoyed the class. The student indicated that he was surprised that the Black teacher did not retaliate for comments made by his father at a parent conference. However, the father consistently wrote defamatory letters during the school year.

There was no relenting, and when conferences and evaluations did not produce the desired results—the removal of a Black classroom teacher—her paycheck was the next target. Amazingly, the timekeeper failed to submit the teacher's payroll records. Paydays are Fridays (bi-weekly), and the teacher noticed she did not receive a direct deposit. Naturally, the teacher inquired, and she is told the problem cannot be resolved until the following Monday. Monday arrives with no solution, and Wednesday, the timekeeper will have an answer. Tuesday, the teacher advanced the matter by contacting the Payroll Office. The office indicates that her records were never submitted. Thinking that this was an oversight by the school's timekeeper, the district payroll office contacted the timekeeper. However, she never returns their phone calls or answers their emails. The Payroll Office gladly generated a check that the teacher picked up Tuesday after school. The school's timekeeper did not convey any updates to the teacher. A Black female administrator later said,..."they want her (the Black teacher) to jump up on a table and act like a monkey...this is what they wanted to see so they could say, I told you so."

So often, the collective and daily interactions with racial microaggressions create a long history associated with degrading the integrity and psychological well-being of Black educators and especially Black female educators in both secondary and collegiate academic environments (Brooks, 2014). When racial aggressions are not implemented, there is always the use of relational aggression, which includes lies, gossiping, and character assassinations that are used to exert power and thus destroy a person's reputation (Morash & Chesney-Lind, 2009).

Black Career Educators, after the *Brown* decision, were blatantly removed from their teaching positions and replaced by white females regardless of their qualifications. When allowed to work in predominantly white school districts with white female teachers, administrators, and principals, Black Career Educators were accused of making white teachers feel threatened or not knowing how to dress as professionals. As if nothing has changed, the same strategy is used toward Black professors (women) in higher education (Black women represent only 2 percent of all full professors in higher education). White females in administrative power positions often target Black women in academia with racialized markers (Daniel, 2018). All in all, white females who engage in racist practices do so with the support of the school's administration and, more importantly, the support of institutional racism.

As an urban sociologist, I define race as a social construct, created by a dominant group to oppress a group of people socially, politically, and economically. Race is not biological but a reality in the social construction of our society and woven throughout the fabric of our nation. When viewed from the perspective of the dominant group, race systemically determines how we view others in society. If you are white, your race is a privilege, but if you are a person of color, you must select a category, one that determines if you are interviewed for a job, used as a statistic to support diversity, qualified to teach white Americans, intellectually challenging, and not a team player who can perpetuate the advancement of white privilege. In the end, as a Black Career Educator, the elements of racism and cultural taxation can destroy your professional environment and discombobulate your mental health.

Racial Macroaggressions in Education

American institutions have historically implemented race-based laws and policies that negatively affect people of color, in particular macroaggressions, which include beliefs and ideologies that are used to structure society according to the interest of the dominant group (Huber & Solorzano, 2014). This collection of ideologies serves as a foundation to justify oppression toward people of color, especially with the use of institutional racism.

In *Brown v. The Board of Education of Topeka* (May 17, 1954), the United States Supreme Court ruled unanimously that, according to the Fourteenth Amendment of the Constitution, racial segregation in public schools was unconstitutional and that separate educational facilities for white and Black students were inherently unequal (dismantling the separate but equal doctrine). At the same time, a decision applying only to public schools, indeed advanced the Civil Rights Movement in the 1950s and 1960s. However, believing that the United States would suddenly transform from a racially segregated nation and desegregate public schools is naive and undermines the power of white supremacy.

Starting at a mid-point, *Brown v. The Board of Education Topeka* and moving to the twenty-first century, macroaggressions represent systemic forms of oppression at the structural level that consistently, over sustained periods, purposefully advance ideologies that support supremacy and power—ideologies that support and justify structures in a society designed by a dominant group that places people of color or non-dominant groups in secondary, dependent, or subservient positions. Macroaggressions, by their very nature, supports racism, including institutional racism, and racial microaggressions.

In other words, when macroaggressions encompass the ideologies of supremacy to maintain power, the concept supports institutional racism, especially as it pertains to education and people of color. The nature of institutional racism is such that it advances the implementation of racial microaggressions and therefore results in the inequality in education as it pertains to children of color.

Desegregating public education in America defied institutional racism, implied the loss of white supremacy and power, and actively invited the creation of macroaggressions to maintain segregation. White supremacy is a disease that supports institutional racism, racism is a symptom of supremacy, and macroaggressions identify the tools used to maintain institutional racism (Huber & Solorzano, 2014).

The desegregation of America's public schools, regardless of what the U.S. Supreme Court states, did not keep state and local school districts from implementing laws, policies, and practices to counter desegregation. In the South, macroaggressions supported the ideologies for segregated schools, housing, and society in general. Institutional racism was enforced with Jim Crow laws and cultivated the formulation of racial microaggressions to oppress people of color, especially Blacks.

Macroaggressions are not new forms of oppression, particularly for Black Americans. Macroaggressions allowed whites to debase millions of Blacks by placing them in segregated ghettoes, segregated schools, and use laws, customs, and government agencies to implement the macroaggressions. Thus, macroaggressions consistently and purposefully dismantled the implementation of *Brown v. The Board of Education of Topeka*. *Brown* could not counteract white supremacy and power as well as racial microaggressions, and achieve education equality. However, *Brown* did perpetuate the belief that Black students and Black teachers were at best inferior to white students and teachers.

In public education, the use of macroaggressions creates a foundation to continue segregation and to counter desegregation policies and laws. According to Jones (2014), southern cities rejected the initial petitions to advance desegregation. Whites retaliated by firing, evicting, and creating other forms of harassment, especially toward Blacks. The state of Alabama outlawed the NAACP. In Arkansas, armed forces were needed to desegregate Little Rock Central High School in 1957. With the use of Jim Crow laws in the South and northern segregation customs, Black students did not encounter equality in public education. In fact, a decade after *Brown*, nearly 91 percent of Black students in the South attended all-Black schools. Over 38,000 Black Career Educators lost their jobs between 1954-1965 (Holmes, 1990; King, 1993). Both outcomes demonstrate the power of southern communities to resist desegregation.

Ironically, Black parents did not need white children to sit next to Black children in public schools. What Black parents needed was access to equality in public education for their children. Nevertheless, whether in the South, West, or North, macroaggressions facilitated desegregation throughout the United States.

The nature of macroaggressions continued after World War II with the support of the Federal Housing Administration facilitating racist practices again targeting people of color, white flight to suburbia, and the abandonment of federal aid to support urban cities and thus advancing urban decline. All these actions further segregated people of color in communities and public schools with the use of racial microaggressions.

The practice of macroaggressions to oppress people of color with the use of institutional racism, economic policies, segregated schools, resegregated schools, elevated levels of unemployment and underemployment, the prison-industrial complex, and environmental racism is alive and well today. Seriously, take note that the resegregation of public education and segregated communities of color in the twenty-first century is identical to before *Brown*, immediately after *Brown*, and continues regardless of superficial gains. According to the Southern Poverty Law Center (2016), the election of Donald Trump advanced racial macroaggressions. Nearly 900 reports of harassment and intimidation were reported within the 10 days following his election. Victims reported physical violence, property damage, hate signs in their front yard, and graffiti on church walls; threats directed at people of color, Jews, and Muslims by supremacist groups, nationalists, and their supporters. All these actions were indicating an open invitation to no longer disguise overt racial hatred and bigotry.

Imagine the impact on students of color in the coming years if supremacists are rallying to "take our country back" and are not afraid to spread hate, violence, and threats inside and outside public schools. Compounded by increases in the wealth gap between whites and people of color, access to equality economically, politically, and socially are eradicating daily.

Racial Microaggressions in Schools

The influence of racial microaggressions at the school district level and in the schoolhouse is evident through policies and operational structures. In urban schools, the evidence points to overcrowding, less qualified teachers, and bias in standardized testing. School districts practice racial microaggressions through academic tracking, disciplinary policies, and the curriculum (Sue et al., 2008).

Compounding the influence of racial microaggressions are socio-cultural influences that leave students feeling a sense of inferiority, which unconsciously affects overall student well-being (Cokley, 2006). With a dramatic increase in the last 10 years suicide rates for both Black and Hispanic students, one can only wonder if racial microaggressions in education are an influence.

Nationwide, the use of zero-tolerance mandates in public schools has increased dropout rates, school suspensions, and expulsions among Black and Hispanic students (American Psychological Association, 2008). Initially, zero-tolerance mandates were a response to school violence, especially gun violence. As time progressed, common infractions such as over-the-counter medications, non-authorized prescriptions, classroom disruptions, insubordination involving teachers and administrators, bullying, and cyber-bullying were added to the list. As a result, school districts experienced an increase in suspension rates and racial discipline gaps for Black and Hispanic students. Historically, marginalized populations encounter harsher consequences than their racial counterparts, a process that perpetuates racial microaggressions in educational settings (Lewis et al., 2010)

The use of curriculum tracking or academic tracking in a school district and school-level policies illustrate the use of racial microaggressions, especially toward Black and Hispanic students. Tracking immediately limits educational access and resources while promoting educational inequalities. According to Allen et al., (2013), students in higher academic tracks usually take advanced courses and apply to four-year colleges. In contrast, students in lower tracks are prepared for vocational training positions and are more likely to drop out of high school. Without question, racial microaggressions impact a student's self-confidence and academic motivation.

A curriculum can reinforce miseducation, especially for marginalized student populations. Imagine a Black and Hispanic school district with a Euro-centered curriculum, a curriculum that provides no indication of African- or Hispanic- centered pedagogy and educators who lack the instructional skills to instruct students of multiple ethnicities. America's majority teaching force encounters a majority population, students of color, so one can only wonder about the level of racial microaggressions toward students of color. These interactions are essential for positive academic outcomes related to students of color as both classrooms, and school climate defines interactions between educators, administrators, and students. The lack of culturally relevant practices invites racial microaggressions, which marginalize students of color (Vega et al, 2012).

A teacher's belief about the students they teach includes assumptions related to abilities and expectations. A teacher's expectations determine culture in a classroom and express an overall tone for academic engagement. Further, primary and secondary educational contexts have the most influence and lasting adverse effects related to racial microaggressions (Rivera, Forquer, & Rangel, 2010). Black male students are more likely to face teachers with racialized beliefs and perspectives about their intelligence, deviance, socioeconomic status, and how they should be disciplined. This belief system drastically influences their ability to use education for social mobility. Even Black male middle-class students reported that teachers saw their behaviors as disrespectful, intimidating, and aggressive (Allen, 2012). Black males in a predominantly white middle-class school, according to Henfield (2011), felt they were criminals and stereotypical caricatures related to Black rappers, gangbangers, and athletes. In the end, white educators must identify their use of racial microaggressions to create nurturing, empathetic, and caring relationships with students of color (Talbert-Johnson, 2006).

Black and Hispanic students facing the negative impact of racial microaggressions are likely to experience issues related to mental health and well-being as both are major effects of racial microaggressions (Nadal, 2010). Racial microaggressions influence a student's psychological functioning, behavior, and build a feeling of inferiority. Racial microaggressions elevate depression, anxiety, trauma, and issues related to self-esteem. Thus, it is not surprising that the impact of racial microaggressions is to cause students of color to perform poorly in standardized tests situations where they are evaluated through the race lens (Cokley, 2006).

If white educators and administrators do not consciously alter racial microaggressions, Black and Hispanic students cannot build cultural wealth through social and navigational capital (Allen, 2012). Without the removal of racial microaggressions, the overall health and intellectual development for the majority population in public schools (students of color) is permanently structured in racism and resegregation, ultimately becoming dismantled.

Racial Microaggressions in Education

One day, I am sitting quietly in an office chair, waiting for the high school counselor's undivided attention in a predominantly white and Jewish all-girls high school—a school that required an entrance exam for the college preparatory program and accepted a limited number of Black students. When the conversation begins, we proceed to discuss career plans as a rising senior. At some point, the white counselor firmly states, "it's a waste of time for you to attend college." Later in life, recounting the conversation, and naturally wondering why she made the statement, I can say that the impact of being a Black girl in a white school environment was compelling. I am the fourth generation of my mother's family to attend Howard University in Washington, DC, and having two college graduate parents with advanced degrees, attending college was not a question of if, but when. However, the counselor comments evaporate in her racist environment, and at the end of my junior year, I left high school to attend

Howard University in the fall.

In 1969, Dr. Chester Pierce, a Black psychiatrist and scholar, introduced the term "offensive mechanisms" (Pierce, 1969). As a scholar, Pierce was interested in the dynamics associated with race and racism in the lives of Blacks. Pierce believed that Blacks experienced a form of social minimizing designed by whites to imply that Blacks were insignificant and irrelevant. In 1970, Dr. Pierce was the first person to introduce the term "microaggression," which he used to explain the more subtle and stunning forms of racism (Pierce, 1970). Thus, Pierce believed that racism was not always gross and crippling but also manifested incessantly, and over time the cumulative effect is unimaginable in magnitude to both the victim and victimizer.

By 1980, Pierce used the term "racial microaggression" to explain the subtle, stunning, repetitive events and dealings of whites to initiate and control Blacks. According to Pierce, the omnipresence of noxious stimuli stood between the social relations of Blacks and whites (Pierce, 1980). In 2000, Pierce reported that racial microaggressions are incredibly stressful for Blacks, and Blacks must recognize, anticipate, evaluate, and dispose of racial microaggressions; otherwise, these innocuous messages continue to devalue Blacks in society and take a cumulative mental toll on Blacks (Profit, 2000). Overall, Pierce determined that the effects of racial microaggressions on people of color caused both negative psychological and physiological implications linked to race-related health consequences.

Racial microaggressions are driven by perceptions that align with dominant cultural beliefs, practices, and policies. Individuals who are members of the dominant group express their social and cultural expressions while gaining power and implying that less dominant groups must conform. The nature of racial microaggressions appears every day in a variety of ways. According to Sue (2010), racial microaggressions can appear in verbal and nonverbal communication, insults, and environmental slights, and are messages that target individuals based on their marginalized status in society.

The following list of examples reported and documented by students, illustrates what is said in classrooms and school environments:

- Failing to learn to pronounce or continuing to mispronounce the names of students after they have corrected you.

- Scheduling tests and project due dates on religious or cultural holidays.

- Disregarding religious traditions or their details. (Ex. Impacts of fasting)

- Setting low expectations for students from particular groups, neighborhoods, or feeder patterns.

- Calling on, engaging with and validating one gender, class, or race of students while ignoring other students during class.

- Assigning student tasks or roles that reinforce particular gender roles or don't allow all students flexibility across roles and responses.

- Anticipating students' emotional responses based on gender, sexual orientation, race or ethnicity.

- Using inappropriate humor in class that degrades students from different groups.

- Using the term "illegals" to reference undocumented students.

- Hosting debates in class that place students from groups who may represent a minority opinion in class in a difficult position.

- Singling students out in class because of their backgrounds.

- Expecting students of any particular group to "represent" the perspectives of others of their race, gender, etc. in class discussions or debates.

- Assigning class projects or creating classroom or school procedures that are heterosexist, sexist, racist, or promote other oppressions, even inadvertently.

- Using sexist language.

- Using heteronormative metaphors or examples in class.

- Assuming the gender of any student.

- Continuing to misuse pronouns even after a student, transgender or not, indicates their preferred gender pronoun.

- Assigning projects that ignore differences in socioeconomic class status and inadvertently penalize students with fewer financial resources.

- Excluding students from accessing student activities due to high financial costs.

- Assuming all students have access to and are proficient in the use of computers and applications for communications about school activities and academic work.

- Dictating whether students of ethnicities must speak another language or must not speak English.

- Complimenting students on their use of "good English."

- Discouraging students from working on projects that explore their own social identities.

- Asking people with hidden disabilities to identify themselves in class.

- Forcing students with non-obvious disabilities to "out" themselves or discuss them publicly.

- Ignoring student-to-student microaggressions, even when the interaction is not course-related.

- Making assumptions about students and their backgrounds.

- Featuring pictures of students of only one ethnicity or gender on the school website.

Reference: Most examples taken, with slight adaptations, from Microaggressions in the Classroom. The University of Denver, Center for Multicultural Excellence, by former students Joel Portman, Tuyen Trisa Bui and Javier Ogaz; and Dr. Jesús Treviño, former Associate Provost for Multicultural Excellence Additional examples from recommended resource: Microaggressions in Everyday Life: Race, Gender, and Sexual Orientation, by Derald Wing Sue, Ph.D.

The consistent influence of racial microaggressions, for Black students, transforms their perception of who is Black, who is successful and Black, and who is allowed to step outside of racial microaggressions. For example, each August or September, I arrived and stood in a classroom to greet students. I appeared darker than a piece of chocolate in front of Black students, and each year indelibly, several students would ask, "What are you...are you mixed." As if I cannot be Black, Articulate, and Clean.

I asked Black students to name someone who was successful because of their academic and cognitive abilities. Students could not include Black individuals who were professionals in sports or entertainment. The room was silent for over 30 seconds when someone said, "Barrack Obama." I had to encourage students to consider Michelle Obama too. Over time, the nature of racial microaggressions takes away the ability to think and form opinions, especially opinions outside of a racially-based cognitive dissonance indoctrination.

The use of racial microaggressions in higher education comes with negative consequences for Black professionals in terms of their mental and physical health. For example, Black college professors represent only 5 percent of faculty members nationwide at predominantly white institutions, and racial microaggressions are significant stressors. In the classroom, faculty meetings, and professional conferences, discriminatory behaviors contribute to emotional and traumatic work environments. Colleagues who believe Black professors can only concentrate on studies related to the African diaspora and students with racialized perceptions of Black faculty members and their intellectual understanding of academic topics outside of the African diaspora, impact evaluations of Black faculty members and overall perceptions. Black faculty members at predominantly white institutions are likely to experience harassing emails, condescendingly comments toward their accomplishments, and often speak about efforts to derail their careers. If academic institutions do not address racial microaggressions, Black educators, especially women in academia will experience toxic classrooms, personal attacks, and hate emails (Young & Hines, 2018).

As for public schools, 80 percent of teachers are white, and most are female. If over 50 percent of public school students are students of color, if 51 percent of students who attend public schools qualify for free or reduced lunch, then how will white teachers avoid racial microaggressions, stereotypes, and other negative alignments when they teach students of color given that racism expressed through racial microaggressions influences an educator's practice, training, and pedagogy?

Without question, racial microaggressions filter into the language, actions, and perceptions of white educators who encounter children of color. Children of color and especially Black children are disproportionately labeled as at-risk, educable mentally retarded, trainable mentally, seriously emotionally disturbed, and developmentally delayed (Ford et al., 1999; Harry & Anderson, 1999; U.S. Department of Education, 2000). Often, white educators assume Blacks students are underachieving even though racially biased assessments misdiagnose them with social, emotional, and behavioral adjustment issues.

The nature of structural racism, regardless of socioeconomic levels, permanently and consistently creates achievement disparities, achievement gaps, removes Black Career Educators from the classroom, establishes resegregated schools, and destroys academic and career links for the future of work for Black and Hispanic students. Even Black middle-class students do not achieve at the level of white middle-class students (Ladson-Billings & Tate, 1995) thus, illustrating the influence of white supremacy and power, and the failure of *Brown* to establish equality in public education.

ABOUT THE AUTHOR

A graduate of Howard University, the author, Dr. Wanda A. Alderman is an urban sociologist and senior consultant. As a senior consultant her focus is on race, diversity, and cultural inclusion. Dr. Alderman is a leading advocate for equality in public education. She lives in Washington, DC, with her husband and their Australian Shepherd, Max. Join her discussions about the current issues related to race, education, and the future of work for students of color. Learn more by visiting her website: lastblackteacher.com Follow her on Facebook, Twitter and Instagram.

References

African Immigration. Library of Congress. (2019). Retrieved from https: www.loc.gov/teachers/classroommaterials/presentationsandactivities/presentations/immigration/alt/african2.html

Alderman-Swain, W., & Battle, J. (2000). The invisible gender: educational outcomes for African American females in father-only versus mother-only households. *Race and Society, 3*(2), 165–182. doi: 10.1016/s1090-9524(01)00027-4

Allen, Q. (2012). "They think minority means lesser than": Black middle-class sons and fathers resisting microaggressions in the school. *Urban Education, 48*(2).

Amadeo, K. (2019). How to Close the Racial Wealth Gap in the United States. Retrieved from https://www.thebalance.com/racial-wealth-gap-in-united-states-4169678

Amemiya, J., & Wang, M.-T. (2018). African American adolescents' gender and perceived school climate moderate how academic coping relates to achievement. *Journal of School Psychology, 69*, 127–142. doi: 10.1016/j.jsp.2018.05.001

American Civil Liberties Union. (2019). Cops and No Counselors. Retrieved from https://www.aclu.org/issues/juvenile-justice/school-prison-pipeline/cops-and-no-counselors

American Federation of Teachers. (2015). Stressed out. Retrieved from https://www.aft.org/periodical/psrp-reporter/fall-2015/stressed-out

American Psychological Association. (2008). Are zero tolerance policies effective in the schools? An evidentiary review and recommendations. Retrieved from https://www.ncbi.nlm.nih.gov/pubmed/?term=American Psychological Association Zero Tolerance Task Force Corporate Author

Anderson, E., Moss, A. A., & Harlan, L. R. (1999). *Dangerous donations northern philanthropy and southern Black education, 1902-1930*. Columbia, Missouri: University of Missouri Press.

Anderson, M., & Jiang, J. (2018). Teens, Social Media & Technology 2018. Retrieved from https://www.pewresearch.org/internet/2018/05/31/teens-social-media-technology- 2018/

Anderson, A., M.D. (2017). Study finds exposure to racism harms children's health. Retrieved from https://www.aappublications.org/news/2017/05/04/P ASRacism050417

Asante, M. K. (2004). *From Imhotep to Akhenaten: An introduction to Egyptian philosophers.* Paris: Menaibuc.

Au, W. W. (2007). Devising inequality: a Bernsteinian analysis of high-stakes testing and social reproduction in education. *British Journal of Sociology of Education, 29*(6), 639–651. doi: 10.1080/01425690802423312

Bailey, J., Bocala, C., Shakman, K., & Zweig, J. (2016). Teacher demographics and evaluation: *A descriptive study in a large urban district (REL 2017–189).* Washington, DC: U.S. Department of Education, Institute of Education Sciences, National Center for Education Evaluation and Regional Assistance, Regional Educational Laboratory Northeast & Islands. Retrieved from http://ies.ed.gov/ncee/edlabs.

Bangura, A. K., & Fenyo, M. D. (2003). *Law and politics at the grassroots: A case study of Prince Georges County.* New York: iUniverse.

Bangura, A. K., & Thomas, A. K. (2011). *Law, politics, and African Americans in Washington, DC.* San Diego, CA: Cognella.

Bankston, C. L., & Pattillo-McCoy, M. (2000). Black Picket Fences: Privilege and Peril among the Black Middle Class. *Contemporary Sociology, 29*(6), 820. doi:10.2307/2654091

Baptiste, N. (2014). Them That's Got Shall Get. Retrieved from https://prospect.org/article/staggering-loss-black-wealth-due-subprime-scandal-continues-unabated

BBC News. (2017). Teachers targeted by cyberbullying pupils and parents. Retrieved from https://www.bbc.com/news/uk-england-devon-14529633

Berliner, D. C. (1986). *In pursuit of the expert pedagogue.* Chicago, IL: Teachem.
Biddle, D., & Dublin, M. (2010). *Tasting Freedom: Octavius Catto and the Battle for Equality i*

Civil War America. Philadelphia, PA: Temple University Press.
Blume, A. W., Lovato, L. V., Thyken, B. N., & Denny, N. (2012). College Student

Microaggression Measure. *PsycTESTS Dataset.* doi: 10.1037/t09884-000

Bonilla-Silva, E. (2015). The Structure of Racism in Color-Blind, "Post-Racial" America. *American Behavioral Scientist, 59*(11), 1358–1376. doi: 10.1177/0002764215586826

Boyd, D., Grossman, P., Ing, M., Lankford, H., Loeb, S., & Wyckoff, J. (2011). The Influence of School Administrators on Teacher Retention Decisions. *American Educational Research Journal, 48*(2), 303–333. doi: 10.3102/0002831210380788

Baker, B. (2018). How Money Matters for Schools. Retrieved from https://learningpolicyinstitute.org/product/how-money-matters-report

Brennan, M., Olaru, D., & Smith, B. (2014). Are exclusion factors capitalized in housing prices? *Case Studies on Transport Policy, 2*(2), 50-60. doi:10.1016/j.cstp.2014.05.002

Bridge, J. A., Horowitz, L. M., Fontanella, C. A., Sheftall, A. H., Greenhouse, J., Kelleher, K. J., & Campo, J. V. (2018). Age-Related Racial Disparity in Suicide Rates Among US Youths From 2001 Through 2015. *JAMA Pediatrics, 172*(7), 697. doi: 10.1001/jamapediatrics.2018.0399

Brooks, J. S., & Arnold, N. W. (2014). *Confronting Racism in Higher Education Problems and Possibilities for Fighting Ignorance, Bigotry and Isolation*. Charlotte: Information Age Publishing.

Broussard, A. (2019). Carlotta Stewart Lai (1881-1952). BlackPast. Retrieved from https://www.blackpast.org/african-american-history/people-african-american-history/lai-carlotta-stewart-1881-1952/

Butchart, R. E. (2010). *Schooling the freed people teaching, learning, and the struggle for black freedom, 1861-1876*. Chapel Hill: The University of North Carolina Press.

Butchart, R. E. (2010). Black hope, white power: Emancipation, reconstruction and the legacy of unequal schooling in the US South, 1861–1880. *Paedagogica Historica, 46*(1-2), 33-50. doi:10.1080/00309230903528447

Butchart, R. E. (2017). Retrieved Freedom Education in Virginia 1861-1870. http://www.encyclopediavirginia.org/Freedmen_s_Education_in_Virginia_1861-1870

Butler, J. S. (1974). Black Educators in Louisiana—A Question of Survival. *The Journal of Negro Education, 43*(1), 9. doi:10.2307/2966937

Calhoun, C. J. (2012). *Contemporary sociological theory*. Wiley-Blackwell.

Campbell., C. (2017). The Medium the Fundamentals of Philosophy.Medium.com

Caplow, T., & Finsterbusch, K. (1964). *A matrix of modernization*. Place of publication not identified.

Carter, J. (2018). W.E.B. DuBois Predicted the Demise of HBCUs Nearly 60 Years Ago. Retrieved from https://hbcudigest.com/w-e-b-dubois-predicted-the-demise-of-hbcus- nearly-60-years-ago/

Castiano, R., & Massey, D. S. (2012). Neighborhood disorder and anxiety symptoms: New evidence from a quasi-experimental study. Retrieved from https://www.ncbi.nlm.nih.gov/pmc/articles/PMC3746323/

Cashin, S. D. (2001, 2005). Middle-Class Black Suburbs and the State of Integration: A Post- Integrationist Vision for Metropolitan America. Retrieved from http://scholarship.law.cornell.edu/cgi/viewcontent.cgi?article=2843&context=clr

Chappell, B., & Kennedy, M. (2019). U.S. Charges Dozens of Parents, Coaches in Massive College Admissions Scandal. Retrieved from https://www.wbur.org/npr/702539140/u-s-accuses-actresses-others-of-fraud-in-wide-college-admissions-scandal

Children in single-parent families by race: KIDS COUNT Data Center. (2018). Retrieved from https://datacenter.kidscount.org/data/tables/107-children-in-single-parent- families-by-race#detailed/1/any/false/37,871,870,573,869,36,868,867,133,38/10,11,9,12,1,185,13/43 2,431

Children's Health Insurance Program (CHIP). (2019). Retrieved from https://www.medicaid.gov/chip/index.html

Civil Rights Data Collection. (2016). Retrieved 2019, from https://ocrdata.ed.gov/ School Based Mental Health

Clark, K. B., & Myrdal, G. (1965). *Dark ghetto*. New York, Evanston and London: Harper & Row.

Clark, K. B. (1967). *Dark ghetto: Dilemmas of social power*. Harper & Row.
Cleveland, R. E., & Sink, C. A. (2017). Student Happiness, School Climate, and School

Improvement Plans. *Professional School Counseling, 21*(1). doi:10.1177/2156759x18761898
Cleveland, R. E., & Sink, C. A. (2017). Student Happiness, School Climate, and School

Improvement Plans. *Professional School Counseling, 21*(1). doi:10.1177/2156759x18761898

Cleveland, R. E., & Sink, C. A. (2017). Student Happiness, School Climate, and School Improvement Plans: Implications for School Counseling Practice - Richard E. Cleveland, Christopher A. Sink. Retrieved from https://journals.sagepub.com/doi/abs/10.1177/2156759X18761898

Clotfelter, C., Orfield, G., & Ashkinaze, C. (1992). The Closing Door: Conservative Policy and Black Opportunity. *Journal of Policy Analysis and Management, 11*(2), 329. doi:10.2307/3325375

Cokley, K. (2006). Institutional racism against African Americans: Physical and mental health implications. In M. G. Constantine & D. W. Sue (Eds.), *Addressing racism: Facilitating cultural competence in mental health and educational settings*. Hoboken, NJ: John Wiley & Sons.

Concentration of Public School Students Eligible for Free or Reduced Prince Lunch. (2018). Retrieved from U.S. Department of Education, National Center for Education Statistics.

Concentration of Public School Students Eligible for Free or Reduced-Price Lunch. (2018). Retrieved from U.S. Department of Education, National Center for Education Statistics. The Condition of Education 2018 (NCES 2018-144)

Constantine, M. G., & Sue, D. W. (2006). *Addressing racism: facilitating cultural competence in mental health and educational settings*. John Wiley & Sons.

Cook, K., Pinder, D., Stewart, S., Uchegbu, A., & Wright, J. (2019). The future of work in black America. Retrieved from https://www.mckinsey.com/~/media/McKinsey/Featured Insights/Future of Organizations/The future of work in black America/The-future-of-work-in-black-America-vF.ashx

Cops and No Counselors. (2019). Retrieved from https://www.aclu.org/report/cops-and-no-counselors

Covitt, M. D. (2012). Lessons from Timbuktu: What Mail's Manuscripts Teach About Peace. Retrieved from https://worldpolicy.org/2012/04/10/lessons-from-timbuktu-what-malis-manuscripts-teach-about-peace/

Cox, C., & Haskins, J. (2000). *African American teachers*. New York: Wiley.

Current Population Survey Annual Social and Economic Supplement. (2019). Retrieved from https://catalog.data.gov/dataset/current-population-survey-annual-social-and-economic-supplement

Danielson, M. N. (1976). *The politics of exclusion*. New York: Columbia University Press.

Data Access and Dissemination Systems (DADS). (2010). American FactFinder - Results. Retrieved from https://factfinder.census.gov/faces/tableservices/jsf/pages/productview.xhtml?src=CF

Davis. (2018). Blacks Are Immune from Mental Illness. Retrieved from https://psychnews.psychiatryonline.org/doi/10.1176/appi.pn.2018.5a18

Deagan, K. A., & MacMahon, D. A. (1995). *Fort Mose: Colonial America's Black Fortress of Freedom*. Gainesville, FL: University Press of Florida.

Department of Assessment and Taxation. (2019). Tax Rates. Retrieved from https://dat.maryland.gov/Pages/Tax-Rates.aspx

Department of Assessment and Taxation. (2019). Assessments: Prince George's County, MD. Retrieved from https://www.princegeorgescountymd.gov/1143/Assessments.

DeVoe, J., Peter, K., Kaufman, P., Ruddy, S., Miller, A., Planty, M., Synder, D., & Rand, M. (2003). Indicators of School Crime and Safety: 2003. Retrieved from https://nces.ed.gov/pubs2004/2004004.pdf

Digest of Education Statistics 2007. (2008). United States Govt. Printing Office. Current expenditure per pupil in average daily attendance in public elementary and secondary schools, by state or jurisdiction: Selected years, 1959-60 through 2004-05. Retrieved from https://nces.ed.gov/programs/digest/

Dreeben, R. (1987). Schooling and Work in the Democratic State. Martin Carney, Henry M. Levin. *American Journal of Sociology, 92*(4), 992-994. doi:10.1086/228596

Du Bois, W. E. B. (1910). The Crisis-NACCP Magazine (1910-1923). Retrieved from http://www.paperlessarchives.com/the_crisis.html

Du Bois, W. E. B. (1973). *The education of Black people: Ten critiques, 1906-1960*. (H. E. B. Aptheker, Ed.). University of Massachusetts Press.

Economic Policy Institute. (2017). *Inequality is slowing US economic growth*. Retrieved from https://www.epi.org/publication/secular-stagnation/

Education and Inspections Act 2006. (2006). Retrieved from http://www.legislation.gov .uk/ukpga/2006/40/contents

Education Bureau Works with Department of Health to Promote Mental Health of Students (2016). Retrieved from https://www .info.gov .hk/gia/general/201608/25/P2016082500387.htm

Education Support Partnership (2016). The mental health and wellbeing charity for education staff. Retrieved from https://www.educationsupportpartnership.org.uk/

Fagell, P. L. (2018). Career Confidential: Principal needs to master art of feedback, not resort to bullying. *Phi Delta Kappan, 100*(3), 68–69. doi: 10.1177/0031721718808271

Fairclough, A. (2002). *Better Day Coming: Blacks and Equality, 1890-2000*. London: Penguin. Fairclough, A. (2004). The Costs of Brown: Black Teachers and School Integration. *Journal of American History, 91*(1), 43. doi:10.2307/3659612

Fairclough, A. (2007). *A Class of Their Own: Black Teachers in the Segregated South*. Harvard University Press.

Fiel, J. E. (2015). *Different sides of the track, or different tracks? socioeconomic disparities in processes of development and educational attainment*. Ann Arbor, MI: ProQuest LLC.

Finn, P. J., & Finn, M. E. (2007). *Teacher education with an attitude: Preparing teachers to educate working-class students in their collective self-interest*. Albany: State University of New York Press.

Fletcher, M. (1998). The Changes: Over 30 Years. *Washington Post Magazine*.
Ford, D. Y. (2015). Culturally Responsive Gifted Classrooms for Culturally Different

Students. *Gifted Child Today, 38*(1), 67–69. doi: 10.1177/1076217514556697
Forten, C. L., & Stevenson, B. E. (1988). *The journals of Charlotte Forten Grimke*. New York: Oxford University Press.

Frankenberg, E. B., Ee, J. B., Ayscue, J. B., & Orfield, G. B. (2019). Harming Our Common Future: America's Segregated Schools 65 Years after Brown. Retrieved from https://www.civilrightsproject.ucla.edu/research/k-12-education/integration-and-diversity/harming-our-common-future-americas-segregated-schools-65-years-after-brown

Frazier, E. F. (1957). *Black bourgeoisie*. Glencoe, Ill: Free Press & Falcons Wing Press.

Friere, P. (2017). *Pedagogy of the Oppressed*. S.l.: Penguin Books.

Fultz, M. (1995). African American Teachers in the South, 1890-1940: Powerlessness and the Ironies of Expectations and Protest. *History of Education Quarterly, 35*(4), 401. doi:10.2307/369578

Gallagher, S. P. (2015). Roger R. Hock, Forty Studies that Changed Psychology: Explorations into the history of psychological research (Global Edition). *Psychology Learning & Teaching, 14*(3), 263–265. doi: 10.1177/1475725715609022

Galt, J. (1848,). Essays on asylums for persons of unsound mind: second series. Retrieved from https://www.worldcat.org/title/essays-on-asylums-for-persons-of-unsound- mind-second-series/oclc/5886095

Garcia-Coll, C. H., Crnic, K. V., Lamberty, G. P., Wasik, B., Jenkins, R., Garcia, H., & Mcadoo, H. (1996). An Integrative Model for the Study of Developmental Competencies in Minority Children. *Child Development, 67*(5), 1891–1914. doi: 10.1111/j.1467- 8624.1996.tb01834.x

Gates, H. (2010). The Trials of Phillis Wheatley: America's First Black Poet and Her Encounters with the Founding Fathers. Civitas Books. New York, New York.

Gilmore, G. E. (2019). *Gender and Jim Crow: Women and the politics of white supremacy in North Carolina, 1896-1920*. Chapel Hill: The University of North Carolina Press.

Goodwill, Engwa. (2014). Science and Technology in Africa: The key Elements and Measures for Sustainable Development. *Global Journal of Science Frontier Research*, 14.

Green, H. (2016). Educational Reconstruction. doi:10.5422/fordham/9780823270118.001.0001

Green, J. G., McLaughlin, K. A., Berglund, P. A., Gruber, M. J., Sampson, N. A., Zaslavsky, A. M., & Kessler, R. C. (2010). Childhood adversities and adult psychiatric disorders in the national comorbidity survey replication I: associations with first onset of DSM-IV disorders. Retrieved from https://www.ncbi.nlm.nih.gov/pmc/articles/PMC2822662/

Green, R. (1998). The empire of Ghana. New York, NY: Grolier Publications.

Hall, C.W. (1953). *A survey of industrial education for Negroes in the United States up to 1917*. Bradley University, Peoria, Illinois.

Haney, J. E. (1978). The Effects of the Brown Decision on Black Educators. *The Journal of Negro Education, 47*(1), 88. doi:10.2307/2967104

Hanushek, E., & Somers, J. (2001). Schooling, Inequality, and the Impact of Government. doi: 10.3386/w7450

Harlem World Magazine: Harlem's Kenneth B. & Mamie Phipps Clark, 1914-2005. (2018). *Harlem World Magazine*.

Harlem's Shifting Population. (2008). *Gotham Gazette*.

Harris Poll Finds Perceived Respect for Teachers Has Declined. (2018). Retrieved from https://theharrispoll.com/new-york-n-y-january-23-2014-with-winter-break-over-and-the-holidays-retreating-into-memory-students-parents-and-teachers-dive-into-the-second-half-of-the-school-year-with-books-back-on-the/

Hartigan, J. (2015). *Race in the 21st Century: Ethnographic approaches*. New York: Oxford University Press.

Haskins, J., Cox, C., & Wilkinson, B. S. (2002). *Black stars of colonial and revolutionary times*. Hoboken, NJ: J. Wiley.

Hattie, J. (2004). Teachers Make a Difference, What is the research evidence? Retrieved from

https://research.acer.edu.au/cgi/viewcontent.cgi?article=1003&context=research_con f erence_2003

Heifetz, J. (2016). Hong Kong's Mental Health Crisis. Retrieved from https://thediplomat.com/2016/06/hong-kongs-mental-health-crisis/

Henfield, M. S. (2011). Black Male Adolescents Navigating Microaggressions in a Traditionally White Middle School: A Qualitative Study. Retrieved from https://onlinelibrary .wiley .com/doi/abs/10.1002/j.2161-1912.2011.tb00147.x

Hock, R. R. (1988). Professional Burnout among Public School Teachers. Retrieved from https://journals.sagepub.com/doi/abs/10.1177/009102608801700207

Holmes, B. J. (1990). *New Strategies are needed to Produce Minority Teachers*. In A. Dorman (Ed.), Recruiting and retaining minority teachers: A national perspective. Elmhurst, IL.: North Central Regional Educational Laboratory.

Holmes, S., & De Witt, K. (1996). Black Successful and Sage and Gone from Capital. *The New York Times*.

Hong Kong Mental Morbidity Survey. (2014). Retrieved from https://www.researchgate.net/publication/261187112_The_Hong_Kong_mental_mor bidity_survey_Background_and_study_design

Housing costs overburden most low income households, especially renters. (2018). doi:10.1787/eco_surveys-grc-2018-graph92-en

Huber, L. P., & Solorzano, D. G. (2014). Racial microaggressions as a tool for critical race research. *Race Ethnicity and Education, 18*(3), 297–320. doi: 10.1080/13613324.2014.994173

Hunter College Libraries: Archives & Special Collections. (1923). Retrieved from https://library.hunter.cuny.edu/archives

Inge, L. (2019). Stagville Historic Site Features Stories of Enslaved Women. Retrieved from https://www.wunc.org/post/stagville-historic-site-features-stories-enslaved-women

Institute for Policy Studies. (2019, September 14). Does the United States Have a 'Strong' Economy? Retrieved from https://ips-dc.org/does-the-united-states-have-a-strong- economy/

Irons, P. H. (2004). *Jim Crows children the broken promise of the Brown decision*. New York, NY.: Penguin Books.

Irvine, J. J. (1991). *Black Students and School Failure. Policies, Practices, and Prescriptions.* Greenwood Press, Inc.

Is School Funding Fair? A National Report Card. (2019). Retrieved from https://edlawcenter.org/assets/files/pdfs/publications/National_Report_Card_2017.pdf

Jackson. (1986). Considering the Possibilities - ASCD. Retrieved from http://www.ascd.org/publications/books/199234/chapters/Considering-the-Possibilities.aspx

Jackson, V. (2002). In Our Own Voices: African American Stories of Oppression, Survival and Recovery in the Mental Health System. *University of Dayton Medical Journal.*

Johnson, J. W. (1992). *Historic U.S. Court cases 1690-1990: an encyclopedia*. New York: Garland.

Johnson, L. (2004). A Generation of Women Activists: African American Female Educators in Harlem, 1930-1950. *The Journal of African American History, 89*(3), 223-240. doi:10.2307/4134076

Johnson, R. (2019). Children of the Dream: Why School Integration Works. Retrieved from https://gspp.berkeley .edu/research/selected-publications/children-of-the-dream- why-school-integration-works

Joint Center for Housing Studies. (2019). The State of the Nation's Housing 2017. Retrieved from https://www.jchs.harvard.edu/research-areas/reports/state-nations-housing- 2017

Jones, B. F. (2014). The Human Capital Stock: A Generalized Approach. Retrieved 2019, from https://www.aeaweb.org/articles?id=10.1257/aer.104.11.3752

Jones, C. (2011). *Must Achievement Gaps Persist? The Struggle for Educational Reform in Prince George's County, Maryland. Must Achievement Gaps Persist? The Struggle for Educational Reform in Prince George's County, Maryland.* Retrieved from https://drum.lib.umd.edu/bitstream/handle/1903/11703/Jones_umd_0117E_12138.p df?sequence=1

Jones, T. J. (1917). *Negro Education, a study of the private and higher schools for colored people in the United States. Prepared in cooperation with the Phelps-Stokes fund under the direction of Thomas Jesse Jones.* Washington: Government Printing Office.

Juergensen, M. (2012). African American Educators' Ideas and Practices for Increasing High School Graduation Rates, 1920-1940. *The Journal of Negro Education, 81*(4), 395. doi:10.7709/jnegroeducation.81.4.0395

Juergensen, M. B. (2015). African American Educators' Ideas and Practices for Increasing High School Graduation Rates, 1920–1940. *The High School Journal, 99*(1), 46-65. doi:10.1353/hsj.2015.0017

Kantrowitz, J., (1970). Education Research Report. Retrieved from https://educationresearchreport.blogspot.com/2018/01/

Keenan-Miller, D., Hammen, C. L., & Brennan, P. A. (2012). Health outcomes related to early adolescent depression. Retrieved from https://www.ncbi.nlm.nih.gov/pmc/articles/PMC2034364/

Kelly, D. (1991). Egyptians and Ethiopians: Color, Race, and Racism. Retrieved from http://www.jstor.org/stable/43936736

Kelly, K., Sullivan, J., & Rich, S. (2015). Broken by the Bubble. *The Washington Post.* KIDS COUNT Data Center. Children in single-parent families. (2014). Retrieved from

https://datacenter.kidscount.org/data/tables/3059-children-in-single-parent-families King, S. H. (1993). The Limited Presence of African-American Teachers. *Review of*

Educational Research, 63(2), 115. doi: 10.2307/1170470
Kirwan Institution for the Study of Race and Ethnicity. (2015). Retrieved from http://kirwaninstitute.osu.edu/

Kishen. (1970). Race of ancient Egyptians. Retrieved from https://kishen-ancientegypt.blogspot.com/2008/02/race-of-ancient-egyptians.html

Knoester, M., & Au, W. (2017). Standardized testing and school segregation: like tinder for fire? *Race Ethnicity and Education, 20*(1), 1–14. doi: 10.1080/13613324.2015.1121474

Kochhar, R., Cilluffo, A., Kochhar, R., & Cilluffo, A. (2017). How U.S. wealth inequality has changed since Great Recession. Retrieved from https://www.pewresearch.org/fact-tank/2017/11/01/how-wealth-inequality-has-changed-in-the-u-s-since-the-great-recession-by-race-ethnicity-and-income/

Kyriacou, C. (1987). Teacher stress and burnout: an international review. *Educational Research, 29*(2), 146–152. doi: 10.1080/0013188870290207

Lapan, R. T., Whitcomb, S. A., & Aleman, N. M. (2012). Connecticut Professional School Counselors: College and Career Counseling Services and Smaller Ratios Benefit Students. *Professional School Counseling, 16*(2). doi:10.1177/2156759x0001600206

Layle Lane, Rights Leader, Teachers' Union Officer, 78. (2017). *The New York Times*.

Lee, J., & Orfield, G. (2006). Tracking Achievement Gaps and Assessing the Impact of NCLB on the Gaps. Retrieved from https://www.civilrightsproject.ucla.edu/research/k-12-education/integration-and-diversity/tracking-achievement-gaps-and-assessing-the-impact-of-nclb-on-the-gaps

Lee, J. (1944). John Robert Edward Lee. *The Journal of Negro History, 29*(3). Published by: The University of Chicago Press on behalf of the Association for the Study of African American Life and History. Retrieved from https://www.jstor.org/stable/2714831

Levy, B. L., Owens, A., & Sampson, R. J. (2019). The Varying Effects of Neighborhood Disadvantage on College Graduation: Moderating and Mediating Mechanisms. *Sociology of Education, 92*(3), 269–292. doi: 10.1177/0038040719850146

Levy, S. (1999). Abstracts. Sixth World Peace Science Congress, Tinbergen Institute, Amsterdam Netherlands, May 24-26, 1999. *Peace Economics, Peace Science and Public Policy, 5*(2). doi:10.2202/1554-8597.1023

Lewis, C. W., Butler, B., Bonner, F., & Joubert, M. (2010). African American male discipline patterns and school district responses resulting impact on academic achievement: Implications for urban educators and policy makers. *Journal of African American Males in Education, 1*(1).

Litwack, L. F. (2006). *Trouble in mind: Black southerners in the age of Jim Crow*. New York: Vintage Books.

Logan, J. R., & Burdick-Will, J. (2017). School Segregation and Disparities in Urban, Suburban, and Rural Areas. *The ANNALS of the American Academy of Political and Social Science, 674*(1), 199–216. doi: 10.1177/0002716217733936

Lopez, W. D., LeBron, A. M., Graham, L. F., & Groan-Kaylor, A. (2014). Discrimination and Depressive Symptoms Among Latina/o Adolescents of Immigrant Parents. *International Quarterly of Community Health Education, 34*(4), 417-419. doi:10.2190/iq.34.4.i

Lucas, J. (2019). Violence Against Teachers is a Silent National Crisis. Retrieved from https://www.ravemobilesafety .com/blog/violence-against-teachers-a-silent-national-crisis

Lyles, M. (2013). *Segregation to Desegregation: The Journey of African American Students to Academia Excellence or Academic Despair* (Doctoral dissertation, University of Washington, Seattle, United States). Retrieved from https://digital.lib.washington.edu/researchworks/bitstream/handle/1773/23634/Lyl es_washington_0250E_11781.pdf?sequence=1

MacAnespie, H. (1978). Mental illness in schoolteachers. *British Medical Journal, 2*(6132), 257–258. doi: 10.1136/bmj.2.6132.257

MacDonald, K. C. (2019). The Road to Timbuktu. Wonders: Sankore Mosque. Retrieved 2019, from https://www.pbs.org/wonders/Episodes/Epi5/5_wondr6.htm

Magirosa, M. (2014). The legacy of Timbuktu, Africa's oldest university. Retrieved from https://www.thepatriot.co.zw/old_posts/the-legacy-of-timbuktu-africas-oldest-university/

Maqbool, M., Sinha, V., & Vikas. (2015). Sustained attention and executive functioning among remitted adolescents with bipolar disorder. *Indian Journal of Psychological Medicine, 37*(3), 322. doi:10.4103/0253-7176.162955

Maqbool, N., Viveiros, J., & Ault, M. (2015, April). The Impacts of Affordable Housing on Health: A Research Summary. Retrieved June 20, 2019, from

https://www .rupco.org/wp-content/uploads/pdfs/The-Impacts-of-Affordable-Housing-on-Health-CenterforHousingPolicy-Maqbool.etal.pdf

Marrast, L., Himmelstein, D. U., & Woolhandler, S. (2016). Racial and Ethnic Disparities in Mental Health Care for Children and Young Adults. *International Journal of Health Services, 46*(4), 810–824. doi: 10.1177/0020731416662736

Mary McLeod Bethune. (2019). Biography. Retrieved from https://www.biography .com/people/mary-mcleod-bethune-921 1266

Maryland Department of Legislative Services, Office of Policy Analysis, 2019. (2019). Retrieved from https://msa.maryland.gov/msa/mdmanual/07leg/legser/html/legser.html

Maryland Minimum Wage. (2019). Retrieved from
https://www.dllr.state.md.us/labor/wages/minimumwagelawpg.pdf

Maryland Poverty Rate County Comparison. (2019). Retrieved from
https://www.welfareinfo.org/poverty-rate/maryland/college-park

Maryland State Department of Education. (2018). Welcome to the Maryland Report
Card. Retrieved from http://reportcard.msde.maryland.gov/

Maryland State Department of Legislative Services, Office of Policy Analysis. (2019).
Retrieved from
http://dls.maryland.gov/pubs/prod/InterGovMatters/LocFinTaxRte/Overview-of-
Maryland-Local-Governments-2019.pdf#search=Prince George's County

Marzano, R. J. (2010). *The art and science of teaching: A comprehensive framework for effective
instruction.* Alexandria, VA: Association for Supervision and Curriculum Development.

Mason, C. N. (2019). Leading at the intersections: An introduction to the intersectional
approach model for policy & social change. Retrieved from
www.intergroupresources.com

Matthews, A. (2017). For the Benefit of these Children: Affirming Racial Identity in the
Era of School Desegregation, Prince George's County, Maryland, 1954-1974 (Master
Thesis, University of Maryland, College Park, United States). Retrieved from
https://drum.lib.umd.edu/bitstream/handle/1903/20444/Matthews_umd_0117N_18
660.pdf?sequence=1&isAllowed=y

McAdoo, H. P. (2002). *Black children: social, educational, and parental environments.* Thousand
Oaks, CA: Sage Publications.

Mckee, J. P., & Jersild, A. T. (1955). Child Psychology. *The American Journal of Psychology,
68*(1), 169. doi: 10.2307/1418412

McNamara, J. (2016, 2019). Prince George's County Council passes $4.1 billion budget.
Retrieved from https://www.capitalgazette.com/maryland/bowie/ac-bb-pg-budget-
0524-story .html

Mental Health and Latino Kids: A Research Review. (2017). Retrieved from
https://salud- america.org/wp-content/uploads/2017/09/FINAL-mental-health-
research-review-9- 12-17.pdf

Mental Illness. (2019). Retrieved from
https://www.nimh.nih.gov/health/statistics/mental-illness.shtml

Milner, H. R., & Howard, T. C. (2004). Black Teachers, Black Students, Black Communities, and Brown: Perspectives and Insights from Experts. *The Journal of Negro Education, 73*(3), 285. doi: 10.2307/4129612

Muhs, Gabriella Gutiérrez y. (2012). *Presumed incompetent: the intersections of race and class for women in academia.* Boulder, CO: University Press of Colorado.

Musu-Gillette, L., Zhang, A., Wang, K., Kemp, J., Diliberti, M., & Oudekerk, B. (2018). Indicators of school crime and safety, Indicators of school crime and safety. Washington, DC: U.S. Dept. of Education, Office of Educational Research and Improvement, National Center for Education Statistics.

Myers, & G., R. (2009). Early Childhood Development Programs in Latin America: Toward Definition of an Investment Strategy. A View from LATHR, No. 32. Retrieved from https://eric.ed.gov/?id=ED369501

Nadal, K. (2010). Gender Microaggressions: Perceptions, Processes, and Coping. *PsycEXTRA Dataset.* doi: 10.1037/e506052012-349

National Assessment of Adult Literacy (NAAL). (1992). Retrieved from https://nces.ed.gov/naal/lit_history .asp

National Center for Education Statistics. (2019). Indicator 6: Status and Trends in the Education of Racial and Ethnic Groups. Retrieved from https://nces.ed.gov/programs/coe/indicator_cge.asp

National Center for Education Statistics (NCES). (2016) U.S. Department of Education. Postsecondary Faculty. Retrieved from https://nces.ed.gov/

National Low Income Housing Coalition (2016). Retrieved from https://nlihc.org/

National Low Income Housing Coalition: The Gap: A Shortage of Affordable Rental Homes (2019). Retrieved June 20, 2019, from https://reports.nlihc.org/sites/default/files/gap/Gap-Report_2019.pdf

National Teacher and Principal Survey (NTPS) (2019). Retrieved from https://nces.ed.gov/surveys/ntps/tables_list.asp

NC Department of Natural Cultural Resources (NCDNCR). (2016). James Walker Hood Died. Retrieved from https://www.ncdcr.gov/blog/2015/10/30/bishop-j-w-hood-of- the-ame-zion-church

Negro Education A Study of the Private and Higher Schools for Colored People in the United States, Volume II. Bulletin, 1916, No. 39. (1917). Washington Government Printing Office. Retrieved from https://files.eric.ed.gov/fulltext/ED542635.pdf

New York African Free School Collection. (2019). Retrieved from https://www .nyhistory .org/web/africanfreeschool/history/

New York Public Library Archives and Manuscripts Layla Lane Papers 1933-1951. (2017). Retrieved from http://archives.nypl.org/divisions/scm/request_access

Neyland, L. W. (1961). Africa: New Frontier for Teaching in Negro Institutions of Higher Learning. *Phylon (1960-), 22*(2), 167. doi:10.2307/273455

Neyland, L. W. (1962). The Educational Leadership of J. R. E. Lee. *Negro History Bulletin, 25*, 75-78.

Noguera, P. A., Pierce, J. C., & Ahram, R. (2014). Race, Education, and the Pursuit of Equality in the Twenty-First Century. *Race and Social Problems, 7*(1), 1–4. doi: 10.1007/s12552-014-9139-9

Noguera, P. (2017). Introduction to Racial Inequality and Education: Patterns and Prospects for the Future. *The Educational Forum.*

Oakley, D., Stowell, J., & Logan, J. R. (2009). The impact of desegregation on black teachers in the metropolis, 1970–2000. *Ethnic and Racial Studies, 32*(9), 1576-1598. doi:10.1080/01419870902780997

OECD: Equity and Quality in Education. (2012). doi: 10.1787/9789264130852-en

Omi, M., & Winant, H. (1986). *Racial formation in the United States.* New York, NY: Routledge.

Omi, M., & Winant, H. (2015). *Racial formation in the United States.* New York, NY: Routledge.

Orfield, G., & Ashkinaze, C. (1991, 1993). *The Closing Door: Conservative Policy and Black Opportunity.* University of Chicago Press.

Orfield, M. (1999). San Diego Metropolitics: A Regional Agenda for Community and Stability. *SSRN Electronic Journal.* doi:10.2139/ssrn.888561

Overview of Maryland Local Governments. (2018). Retrieved from http://dls.maryland.gov/pubs/prod/InterGovMatters/LocFinTaxRte/Overview-of-Maryland-Local-Governments-2018.pdf

Page, T. (2017). DNA discovery unlocks secrets of ancient Egyptians. Retrieved from https://www.cnn.com/2017/06/22/health/ancient-egypt-mummy-dna-genome-heritage/index.html

Patten, E. (2016). The Nation's Latino Population Is Defined by Its Youth. Retrieved from https://www.pewhispanic.org/2016/04/20/the-nations-latino-population-is-defined- by-its-youth/

Pattillo, M., & Lareau, A. L. (2013). *Black picket fences: privilege and peril among the black middle class.* The University of Chicago.

Pattillo-McCoy, M. (1998). *The invisible black middle class.* Evanston, IL: Institute for Policy Research, Northwestern University.

Pierce, C. (1970). Offensive Mechanism. In the Black Seventies, edited by R. Barbour. Boston, MA: Porter Sargent.

Pierce, C. (1980). Social Trace Contaminants: Subtle Indicators of Racism in TV. In Television and Social Behaviors: Beyond Violence and Children, edited by S. Wither and R. Abeles. Hillsdale, NY: Lawrence Erlbaum.

Pierce, C. (1969). Is Bigotry the Basis of the Medical Problem of the Ghetto? In Medicine in the Ghetto, edited by J. Norman. New York: Meredith Corporation.

Pirog, M. (2017). TANF and SNAP Asset Limits and the Financial Behavior of Low-Income Households. Retrieved from https://www.pewtrusts.org/-/media/assets/2017/09/tanf_and_snap_asset_limits_and_the_financial_behavior_of_low_income_households.pdf

Population of Charles County, Maryland: Census 2010 and 2000 Interactive Map, Demographics, Statistics, Graphs, Quick Facts. (2019). Retrieved from http://censusviewer.com/county/MD/Charles

Poverty in America. (2019). Poverty and Equity: Thought Leadership on SaportaReport. Retrieved from https://leadership.saportareport.com/povertyandequity/2019/01/28/poverty-in-america/

Poverty in America: Prince George's County, Maryland. (2019). Retrieved from http://welfareresearch.org/povertyrates

Prince George's County. (2019). Population Data. Retrieved from http://worldpopulationreview.com/us-counties/md/prince-georges-county-population/

Profit, W., Mino, I., & Pierce, C. (2000). Blacks Stress. In *Encyclopedia of Stress.* San Diego, CA: Academic Press.

Reardon, S. F., & Owens, A. (2014). 60 Years After Brown: Trends and Consequences of School Segregation. *Annual Review of Sociology, 40*(1), 199-218. doi:10.1146/annurev-soc- 071913-043152

Renner, B., Renner, A. B., & Ben, V. (2019). Study: Suicide Rates Rising Rapidly Among African American Teens. Retrieved from https://www.studyfinds.org/suicide-rates- rising-rapidly-among-african-american-teens/

Riggio, R. (2017). Are Teachers Getting Bullied? Retrieved from https://www.psychologytoday .com/ca/blog/cutting-edge-leadership/20171 1/are-teachers-getting-bullied

Robertson, S., White, S., & Garton, S. (2013). Harlem in Black and White: Mapping Race and Place in the 1920s. Retrieved from https://journals.sagepub.com/doi/abs/10.1177/0096144213479309

Roosevelt Institute: Reimagine the Rules (2016). Retrieved from https://www.rooseveltboston.org/

Rosales, J. (2019). The Racist Beginnings of Standardized Testing. Retrieved from http://www.nea.org/home/73288.htm

Rothenberg, P. S. (2012). *White privilege: Essential readings on the other side of racism*. New York: Worth. Retrieved from https://www.amazon.com/White-Privilege-Paula-S-Rothenberg/dp/1429242205

Rothstein, R. (2017). *The color of law: A forgotten history of how our government segregated America*. Liveright publishing corporation, a division of W. W. Norton & Company.

Rudd, T. (2019). Who you calling minority? The imperative to improve educational opportunity for the nation's emerging majority. Retrieved from http://kirwaninstitute.osu.edu/author/trudd/

Russell, D. (2019). Staff wellbeing: Teacher targeted bullying and harassment. Retrieved from https://www.teachermagazine.com.au/articles/staff-wellbeing-teacher-targeted-bullying-and-harassment

Sampson, R. J., Morenoff, J. D., & Gannon-Rowley, T. (2002). Assessing "Neighborhood Effects": Social Processes and New Directions in Research.*Annual Review of Sociology, 28*(1), 443–478. doi: 10.1146/annurev.soc.28.110601.141114

Saporito, S. & Lareau, A. (1999). School Selection as a Process: The Multiple Dimensions of Race in Framing Educational Choice. Social Problems 46, no. 3, 418-39. Doi:10.2307/3097108

Sarah E. Goode. (2019). Biography. Retrieved from http://www .biography .com/inventor/sarah-e-goode

Schomburg Center for Research in Black Culture: WWII, Housing, and Politics. (2017). Retrieved from https://blacknewyorkers-nypl.org/education/

Sellgren, K. (2016). Warning over state of teachers' mental health. Retrieved from https://www.bbc.co.uk/news/education-35900499

Shorton, A. (2014). International Comparison of the Teacher Environment – Report on the Results of the Oecd Teaching and Learning International Survey (Talis) 2013. Edited by the National Institute for Education Policy Research.

Silcox, H. (1973). Philadelphia Negro Educator: Jacob C. White, Jr., 1837-1902. *The Pennsylvania Magazine of History and Biography*. Retrieved from https://www.jstor.org/stable/20090708?seq=1#page_scan_tab_contents

Simpson, D., Jackson, M., & Aycock, J. (2007). John Dewey and the Art of Teaching: Toward Reflective and Imaginative Practice. *Teaching Theology & Religion, 11*(1), 55-57. doi:10.1111/j.1467-9647.2007.00398.x

Singh, G. K., & Ghandour, R. M. (2012). Impact of Neighborhood Social Conditions and Household Socioeconomic Status on Behavioral Problems Among US Children. *Maternal and Child Health Journal, 16*(S1), 158–169. doi: 10.1007/s10995-012-1005-z

Singhal, P. (2017). Teacher awarded six-figure payout after being bullied by school principal. Retrieved from https://www.smh.com.au/education/teacher-awarded-sixfigure-payout-after-being-bullied-by-school-principal-20170919-gyk761.html

Skinner. (2015). The Manuscripts of Timbuktu; The Meanings of Timbuktu; 333 Saints: A Life of Scholarship in Timbuktu. *Journal of West African History*, 1(1), 195. doi:10.14321/jwestafrihist.1.1.0195

Smithsonian. (2019). Quest for Education. Retrieved from https://americanhistory .si.edu/brown/history/2-battleground/quest-for-education-2.html

Snowden, F. M. (1970). *Blacks in antiquity; Ethiopians in the Greco-Roman experience.* Cambridge, MA: Belknap Press of Harvard University Press.

Sorokin, P. A. (1962). *Social and cultural dynamics.* New York: Bedminster Press.

Sorokin, P. A. (1973). *Man, and society in calamity: The effects of war, revolution, famine, pestilence upon human mind, behavior, social organization and culture life*. Westport, Conn: Greenwood Press.

Southern Poverty Law Center. (2016). The Trump Effect: The Impact of the 2016 Presidential Election on Our Nation's Schools. (2016). Retrieved from https: ??www.splcenter.org/

Stacciarini, J., Smith, R., Garvan, C. W., Wiens, B., & Cottler, L. B. (2015). Rural Latinos' Mental Wellbeing: A Mixed-methods Pilot Study of Family, Environment and Social Isolation Factors. *Community Mental Health Journal, 51*, 404–413

Staff, S. I. (2018). International Schools: What is a British-based curriculum? Retrieved from https://www.studyinternational.com/news/british-based-curriculum-what- does-it-mean/

Stagman, S., & Cooper, J. (2010). Children's Mental Health: What Every Policymaker Should Know. Retrieved from https://www.scirp.org/(S(i43dyn45teexjx455qlt3d2q))/reference/ReferencesPapers.as px?ReferenceID=1186308

State of Urban Connecticut 2019-Digital Copy. (2019). Retrieved from https://www.ulsc.org/s019report/state-of-urban-connecticut-2019-digital-copy

Subramaniam, M., Vaingankar, J., Heng, D., Kwok, K. W., Lim, Y. W., Yap, M., & Chong, S. A. (2012). The Singapore Mental Health Study: an overview of the methodology. *International Journal of Methods in Psychiatric Research, 21*(2), 149–157. doi: 10.1002/mpr.1351

Sue, D. W., Nadal, K. L., Capodilupo, C. M., Lin, A. I., Torino, G. C., & Rivera, D. P. (2008). Racial Microaggressions Against Black Americans: Implications for Counseling. *Journal of Counseling & Development, 86*(3), 330–338. doi: 10.1002/j.1556-6678.2008.tb00517.x

Sue, D. W. (2010). *Microaggressions in everyday life: race, gender and sexual orientation*. Hoboken: NJ. John Wiley & Sons.

Talbert-Johnson, C. (2006). Preparing Highly Qualified Teacher Candidates for Urban Schools. *Education and Urban Society, 39*(1), 147–160. doi: 10.1177/0013124506293321

TALIS - The OECD Teaching and Learning International Survey. (2016). Retrieved from http://www.oecd.org/education/talis/

TANF and SNAP Asset Limits and the Financial Behavior. (2017). Retrieved from https://www.pewtrusts.org

Taylor, K. (2017). Poverty's Long-Lasting Effects on Student's Education and Success. Retrieved from https://www.insightintodiversity.com/povertys-long-lasting-effects-on-students-education-and-success/

Terrell, M. C. (1917). History of the High School for Negroes in Washington. Retrieved from https://www.jstor.org/stable/2713767

The Mainichi Newspaper. (2016). Over 5,000 teachers in Japan took sick leave for mental illness in 2015 school year. Retrieved from https://mainichi.jp/english/articles/20161223/p2a/00m/0na/006000c

The New Foundational Skills of the Digital Economy. (2019). Retrieved from https://www.burning-glass.com

The Singapore Mental Health Study: An overview of the methodology. (2016). Retrieved from

https://www.researchgate.net/publication/221829860_The_Singapore_Mental_Health_Study_An_overview_of_the_methodology

The Southern Manifesto of 1956. (1956). Retrieved from http://history.house.gov/Historical-Highlights/1951-2000/The-Southern-Manifesto-of-1956/

Thornton, A., & Gooden, K. L. W. (1997). *Like a phoenix I'll rise: An illustrated history of African Americans in Prince Georges County, Maryland, 1696-1996.* Upper Marlboro, MD: Pyramid Visions.

Tokyo Times, (2011). Why Japanese teachers quit. Retrieved from https://educationinjapan.wordpress.com/edu-news/why-japanese-teachers-quit/

Tolmacheva, M., Hamdun, S., & King, N. (1995). Ibn Battuta in Black Africa. *The International Journal of African Historical Studies, 28*(3), 696. doi:10.2307/221221

Travers, R. M., & Gage, N. L. (1973). *Handbook of research on teaching: A project of the American Educational Research Association.* Rand McNally.

Tyack, D. (1974). *The One Best System: A History of American Urban Education.* Cambridge, MA: Harvard University Press.

U.S. Census 2017 American Community Survey 5-Year Data. (2017). Retrieved from http://census.hawaii.gov/whats-new-releases/2017-american-community-survey-5-year-data/

U.S. Census 2018. Annual Estimates of the Resident Population. (n.d.). Retrieved from Annual Estimates of the Resident Population: April 1, 2010 to July 1, 2018 Source: U.S. Census Bureau, Population Division.

U.S. Census Bureau. (2005). Census 1990, 2005 U.S. Census Bureau Population Estimates. Retrieved from https://www.census.gov/

U.S. Census Bureau. (2010a). Data Access and Dissemination Systems (DADS). (2010). American FactFinder. Retrieved from https://factfinder.census.gov/faces/nav/jsf/pages/community_facts.xhtml?src=bkmk

U.S. Census Bureau, Small Area Income and Poverty Estimates. (2010b). Retrieved from https://factfinder.census.gov/bkmk/table/1.0/en/ACS/17_5YR/DP05/0100000US

U.S. Census Bureau. (2016a). Poverty in Bladensburg, Maryland. Retrieved from https://www.welfareinfo.org/poverty-rate/maryland/bladensburg

U.S. Office of Minority Health, Mental Health and Hispanics (2016b). Retrieved from https://minorityhealth.hhs.gov/Default.aspx

U.S. Department of Education. (2017a). Study shows preschool suspensions a huge problem. Retrieved from https://www.wxyz.com/news/us-dept-of-education-study-shows-preschool-suspensions-a-huge-problem

U.S. Department of Education. (2017b). Homeless Student Enrollment Data by Local Educational by Local Education Agency. Retrieved from https://www2.ed.gov/about/inits/ed/edfacts/data-files/lea-homeless-enrolled-sy2015-16-public-file-documentation.doc

U.S. Census Bureau. (2017c). SNAP Benefits Recipients in Prince George's County, MD. Retrieved from https://alfred.stlouisfed.org/release?rid=346

U.S. Census Bureau. (2017d). SNAP Benefits Recipients in Prince George's County Maryland. Retrieved from U.S. Census Bureau, SNAP Benefits Recipients in Prince George's County, MD [CBR24033MDA647NCEN], retrieved from FRED, Federal Reserve Bank of St. Louis; https://fred.stlouisfed.org/series/CBR24033MDA647NCEN, July 17, 2019

U.S. Census Bureau. (2017e). Census Bureau: Small Area Income and Poverty Estimates for Counties. Retrieved from https://www.learncra.com/census-bureau-small-area- income-and-poverty-estimates-for-counties/

U.S. Census Bureau QuickFacts: United States. (2018a). Retrieved from https://www.census.gov/quickfacts/fact/table/US/PST045218

U.S. Census Bureau. (2018b). Small Area Income and Poverty Estimates (SAIPE) Program. Retrieved from https://www.census.gov/programs-surveys/saipe.html

U.S. Census Bureau. (2018c). Census.gov. Retrieved from https://www.census.gov/search-results.html?q=bladensburg, Maryland&page=1&stateGeo=none&searchtype=web&cssp=SERP&_charset_=UTF-8

U.S. Census Bureau. (2019a). American Community Survey (ACS). Retrieved from https://www.census.gov/programs-surveys/acs/

U.S. Census Bureau. (2019b). American Community Survey (ACS). Retrieved from https://www.census.gov/programs-surveys/acs/

U.S. Census Bureau QuickFacts: United States. (2019c). Retrieved from https://www.census.gov/quickfacts/fact/table/US/PST045218

U.S. Census Bureau. (2019d). American FactFinder - Results. Retrieved from https://www.census.gov/search-results.html?q=college park, maryland&page=1&stateGeo=none&searchtype=web&cssp=SERP&_charset_=UTF-8

U.S. Census Bureau. (2019e). QuickFacts: Prince George's County, Maryland. Retrieved from https://www.census.gov/quickfacts/princegeorgescountymaryland

U.S. Census Bureau. (2019f). U.S. Census City/Town Population estimates - Most recent state estimates from the Census Bureau's Population Estimates Program Population of States and Counties of the United States: 1790 - 1990. Retrieved from https://www.census.gov/

Umeh, U. (2019). Mental Illness in Black Community, 1700-2019: A Short History BlackPast. Retrieved from https://www.blackpast.org/african-american-history/mental-illness-in-black-community-1700-2019-a-short-history/

United States Commission on Civil Rights Home Page. (1965). Retrieved from https://www.usccr.gov/

Valencia, R. R. (1996). The Evolution of Deficit Thinking: Educational Thought and Practice. The Stanford Series on Education and Public Policy. Retrieved from https://eric.ed.gov/?id=ED413139

Valien, P. (1955). The Desegregation Decision--One Year Afterward--A Critical Summary. *The Journal of Negro Education, 24*(3), 388. doi: 10.2307/2293468

Vegas, D., Forquer, E., & Rangel, R. (2010). Microaggressions and the life experiences of Latina/o Americans. In *Microaggressions and marginally: Manifestation, dynamics, and impact*. Hoboken, NJ: Wiley.

Vegas, D., Moore, J., Baker, C., Bowen, N., Hines, E., O'Neal, B., & Lewis, C. (2012). Salient factors affecting urban African American students' achievement: Recommendations for teachers, school counselors, and school psychologists. In *African American students in urban schools: Critical issues and solutions for achievement*. New York, NY: Peter Lang.

Walker, R. (2018). As Suicide Rates for Black Children Rise, Protecting Emotional Heath Is Vital. Retrieved from https://www.ebony.com/health/black-suicide-rates/

Walker, V. S. (2000). Valued Segregated Schools for African American Children in the South, 1935-1969: A Review of Common Themes and Characteristics. *Review of Educational Research, 70*(3), 253. doi:10.2307/1170784

Walker, V. S. (2001). African American Teaching in the South: 1940–1960. *American Educational Research Journal, 38*(4), 751-779. doi:10.3102/00028312038004751

Walker, V. S. (2017). Black Schools in the Segregated South. *Encyclopedia of Diversity in Education*. doi:10.4135/9781452218533.n81

Welfare. (2019). Poverty Rate, Maryland, and Prince George's County, Maryland. Retrieved from https://www.welfareinfo.org/poverty-rate/maryland/prince-georges-county

Wells, A. S. (2018). The Process of Racial Resegregation in Housing and Schools: The Sociology of Reputation. In R. A. Scott & M. Buchmann (Eds.), *Emerging Trends in the Social and Behavioral Sciences*. John Wiley & Sons.

White, I. (2019). Racial Differences on the Future of Work: A Survey of the American Workforce. Retrieved from https://jointcenter.org/sites/default/files/Joint Center - Racial Differences on the Future of Work - A Survey of the American Workforce_0.pdf

Williams, J. J. (1946). Women in the Professions: A Wartime Survey: A Study Made Cooperatively by the Research Division of the National Education Association and the Committee on Studies and Awards of Pi Lambda Theta. Research Division of the National Education Association, Committee on Studies and Awards of Pi Lambda Theta. *American Journal of Sociology, 52*(1), 82-83. doi:10.1086/219945

Willie, C. V., Garibaldi, A. M., & Reed, W. L. (1991). *The Education of African-Americans*. New York: Auburn House.

Wong, C. A., Eccles, J. S., & Sameroff, A. (2003). The Influence of Ethnic Discrimination and Ethnic Identification on African American adolescents School and Socioemotional Adjustment. *Journal of Personality, 71*(6), 1197-1232. doi:10.1111/1467-6494.7106012

Woodson, C. G. (1915). *The Education of the Negro prior to 1861, etc.* Pp. v. 454. G.P. Putnam's Sons: New York & London.

Woodson, C. G. (1933). *The mis-education of the Negro.* Washington, DC: The Associated Publishers.

Yoshida, H. (2013). States Move to Protect Teachers from Cyberbullying. News and Features from the National Education Association. Retrieved from http://neatoday .org/2013/07/24/states-move-to-protect-teachers-from-cyberbullying- 2/

Young, J. L., & Hines, D. E. (2018). Killing My Spirit, Renewing My Soul: Black Female Professors Critical Reflections on Spirit Killings While Teaching. *Women, Gender, and Families of Color, 6*(1), 18. doi: 10.5406/womgenfamcol.6.1.0018

Yurco, F. (1989). Were the Ancient Egyptians Black or White. *Biblical Archaeology Review.*

Index

A

African diaspora, 11, 127
African Free School, 13
African Methodist Episcopal
    Zion Church, 14
American Civil War, 12
American Educators Association
    Bulletin, 16-17
American Federation of Teachers, 20,
42

American Missionary Association
(AMA), 12
Amsterdam News, 19
Angelou, Maya, 52
Antisocial behavioral problems, 50,
58-59
Apartheid schools, 95
Ayer, Elise McDougald, 19-21

B

Benin, 10
Bishop College, 17
Black childhood traumas, 52
Black churches, 14
Black employment, 103
Black families, vi, 50-51, 79-82, 85, 94,
97-98, 100

Black suburban enclave, 94, 99-100,
103
Black youth, 27, 49
Boise, Louise Metoyer, 21
Bond, Horace Mann, 21-22
British education system, 44

British Parliament, 11
British teachers, 43
Brown, Claude, 51
Brown, Henry B., 22
Brown v. Board of Education,
iii-iv, viii, 9, 14, 20, 22-23, 25-26, 28-29,
38, 45, 51-52, 79, 95, 111-113, 118-121,
128
Bullying, v, 53, 60-61, 66-67, 69, 72-73,
122

C

Castillo de San Marcos, 10
Catto, Octovius Valentine, 17
Charles County, Maryland, 95
Chavis, John, 11
Cheyney University, 17
Civil Rights Movement, 24, 26, 107,
115

Civil War, 12-17, 21-22, 45-46
Clark, Kenneth, 74-75
Clark, Mamie Phipps, 74
College admissions scandal, 84
Colored schools, 17, 74
Columbine High School, 59
Colyer, Vincent, 17

Common slang, 57
Community Reinvestment Act, 94
Cooper, Anna Julia Haywood, 16
Criminalization, ii, 36, 38-40, 49, 55
Cugoano, Quobna Ottobah, 111

Curriculum, 19-20, 24, 30, 39, 42, 44,
65, 73, 87 102, 108, 110, 117-118

Cyberbullying, iv, 61, 70-71

D

Deficit thinking, iii-iv, 49, 88, 91
Desegregate public schools, 28, 78
Desegregation, iii-iv, 24-26, 79, 93-97, 120-121
Dewey, John, 3

Diodorus Siculus, 9
Diop, Cheeks Anta,
Disenfranchised, iv, 8, 55
Disruptive behaviors, iv, 61

E

Economic empowerment, 101
Economic inequalities, 6, 19, 39, 77, 94
Economic policies, 45, 50, 117
Educational attainment, 6, 29-30, 83-84, 99
Educational policies, 39, 51, 78, 113
Educators Union of New York City, 19-20

Elementary and Secondary Education Act, 86
Epidemic poverty levels, 55, 103
Equal Credit Opportunity Act, 94
Equiano, Olaudah, 11

Estevanico, 10
Eudoxus, 9
Every Student Succeeds Act, 86

F

Fair Housing Act, 48, 98

Fairwood, 96
Ferguson, Catherine Williams, 13,
Federal Housing Authority (FHA), 94
FHA's Underwriting Manual, 94
Fifteenth Amendment, 17, 22

Florida Agricultural and Mechanical University, 16-17

Fort Mose, 10
Forten, Charlotte, 13
Fourteenth Amendment, 22, 115
Free and reduced lunch, 92
Freedmen Bureau, 12-13
Freire, Paulo, 5

Future of work, ii, v, 6, 27, 30, 36, 39-40, 55, 77, 82, 98-99, 103-104, 109, 124

G

Gentrification, 82, 85, 112
Georgetown University, 111
Ghana, 9, 11
Great Depression, 19-20, 23

H

Harlem, 18-20, 51, 74
Harlem Riot, 19
Healy, Patrick Francis, 111
Hispanic/ children/students, iv, 28, 37, 53-54, 81, 83-84, 87-88, 92-93, 95, 101-102, 106, 113, 122, 123
Hood, James Walker, 14
Housing discrimination, 75, 77
Housing segregation, 26, 75-78, 80, 89

Howard University, 15, 20, 112, 119-120

Hunt, Ida Gibbs, 16
Hunter College, 20

I

Inequalities in segregated public
schools, 53
Innatism, 2
Institute for Colored Youth, 17
Institutional racism, vii, 29, 47, 49, 52,
77-78, 80, 90, 93, 111, 113, 119-120
Intimidating teachers, 60, 114

J

Japanese teachers, 44
Jim Crow, 15, 18, 21-25, 27, 81,
113, 120
Johnson, Peter A., 20

L

Lane, Layla, 19-20
Lee, John Robert Edward, 17
Life-sustaining employment, iii, vi, 6,
29, 55, 77, 79, 87, 97, 104

Low wages, 101
Low-income, vii, 5-7, 36, 48-49, 53, 80-
81, 84-86, 89-91, 96, 98, 101, 103-107,
112-113

Low-income communities, 105, 135,
141
Low-income families, vi, 30, 49, 76-77,
81, 84-85, 94, 101, 108

M

M Street High School, 16
Macroaggressions, 114, 119-121
Mali, 9-10
Marginalized, v, vii, 6, 8, 37, 113, 122
Marginalized students, 37
Marijuana, v-vi, 35, 73-74
Marshall, Supreme Court Justice
Thurgood, 20
Maryland Comprehensive Assessment
    Program, 101

Mason, Rev. John Mitchell, 13
Massachusetts Supreme Court, 15
McGrawville College, 13
McLeod Bethune, 16
Marzano, Robert, 2-3

Medicaid and Children's Health
    Insurance Program, 51

Mental breakdowns, 41, 43, 55
Mental disorders, 43, 45, 47
Mental health, iv, vi, 29, 34, 36-38,
41-48, 50-55, 83, 119, 123

Mental health inequalities, 47
Mental stress, 47, 49, 41
Microaggressions, 108, 110-111, 114,
116-120
Morris, Robert, 15
Multigenerational poverty, 50
Murray Street Sabbath School, 13

N

National Association for the
Advancement of Colored People
(NAACP), 24, 74
National Association of Educators in
Colored Schools, 23

Wilson, Mary Jane, 16
Woodson, Carter G., 12, 23, 28
World War II, 25, 117
Wright, Richard, 51

Z

Zero-tolerance mandates, 52, 122

Made in the USA
Middletown, DE
10 April 2020